LOVE
yourself
HAPPY

A JOURNEY BACK TO YOU

Praise for *Love Yourself Happy*

"*Love Yourself Happy* is a powerful, compassionate voice for self love that will convince you it's the answer; the one best secret to living an authentic, joyful, purposeful life. The author leads us on a journey back to ourselves and has us loving her, ourselves and the whole darn process along the way. With humor and genuine kindness this book helps us into the pain so we can fall in love with all of who we are and get on with living our best possible life. If you love books by super-positive, in-it-for-the-healing, badass people, like I do, buy this one!"

— **Laura Di Franco**, MPT, Author of *Brave Healing, a Guide for Your Journey*

"Through humor, compassion and a daring authenticity, Shari expertly weaves her life's journey with life lessons and takes us along with her for the ride. It's like hanging out with your best friend and going on fun adventures filled with insight and wisdom. *Love Yourself Happy* is about the totality of who we are in all moments—and the full loving acceptance of who we are and how we show up in the world. Poignant, touching and inspiring! A must read for anyone who has ever wanted to love themselves more."

— **Dr. Debi Silber**, Founder of The PBT (Post Betrayal Transformation) Institute.

"Shari Alyse guides you with insight, humor, and heart through her journey to reunite with her soul and on the way, she opens the way for your own soulful discovery."

— **Elizabeth Kipp**, Health Practitioner and Author of *The Way through Chronic Pain*

"For all of us that think we are a hot mess or crazy, Shari's story, which is nearly impossible to put down, will show you, you are not alone. We are all human and we all can be happy. Thank you for the guidance Shari and sharing your messy turned inspiring journey with us. Life is life! Thank you for being so real, giving us hope and a guide to self-love and happiness. Perfection!"

– **Anna Pereira**, Founder of The Wellness Universe

"Since self-love is my personal passion and professional mission, I'm very well versed in the various books and approaches out there. I particularly love this one because Shari Alyse has a beautiful vulnerability combined with a profound trust in her connection to the divine, which really speaks to my soul. Shari takes us on a journey that reminds us that no matter what road we might travel down, it's all okay and it's all beautiful—even the hard stuff. This love-filled book felt like a delicious hug for my soul. I will recommend it to my clients!"

– **Jasmin Terrany**, LMHC, Helping High Achievers Be Successful in their Personal-Lives Too. www.JasminTerrany.com.

"Through, *Love Yourself Happy*, Shari Alyse is telling everyone's story. Yes, the characters are different, events and experiences different, and yet we each move through experiences of doubt, fear, judgment, unworthiness, rejection, pain, love and so on. *Love Yourself Happy* will help you cleanse the many layers of untruths you have accepted and attend to about your Self, revealing the Truth that you are, have been and always will be a Divine Being. Most of us will never boldly put our stories out there for the world to see, however we must be bold enough to clearly see it for ourselves. As Shari so succinctly states, "the greatest love story ever told is the one that begins with me. " Embrace your Self as you embrace the message of this wonderful book."

– **Jim Phillips**, Author of *The Key to LIFE; living in full expression* and *"From Inspiration to Intention."*

"If you're ready to positively transform your life, then follow the strategies in this brilliant book by my friend Shari Alyse! Shari truly cares about helping others, and her philosophies and ideas will make a powerful, positive difference in your life!"

— **Diane Forster**, Intentional Living Expert; Mindset & Manifestation Mentor; TV Host-Podcaster-Keynote Speaker-Inventor; Best Selling Author and Founder—I Have Today

"*Love Yourself Happy* is an incredibly real, raw and beautiful book about how to journey back to the most important person, you. Shari Alyse takes you on a personal adventure into the spaces and places that can trouble and upset us most, yet she shows you how to love yourself through it all to experience a life that is a heck of a lot more peaceful, sweeter and loving. This is a journey not to miss."

— **Julie Reisler**, Author, Speaker, Podcast Host, Life Designer® | juliereisler.com

"*Love Yourself Happy* is more than a journey to help you find happiness, it's a deep, soulful journey to discover who you truly are—a precious soul meant to shine. From the moment I met Shari, I was taken by her amazing enthusiasm and zest for life. I later discovered the trauma she transcended to become the light she is today. In this wonderful book, Shari reminds us that all of life's chapters begin and end with love when you write them from your heart. This book is a must read!"

— **Robert Clancy**, Bestselling Author of *Soul Cyphers*, and Co-Host of The Mindset Reset Show

SHARI ALYSE

LOVE *yourself* HAPPY

A JOURNEY BACK TO YOU

WELLNESS INK PUBLISHING

Love Yourself Happy
A Journey Back to You

By Shari Alyse

 Wellness Ink Publishing
www.WellnessInk.com

ISBN: 978-1-988645-29-2 (paperback) | 978-1-988645-30-8 (digital)

Publishing services provided by:

Contact Shari Alyse:
Email: Shari@ShariAlyse.com
Website: www.ShariAlyse.com

DEDICATION

This book is a love letter to your soul.
Dedicated to your shadows.
Loving yourself through them, in spite
of them and because of them.

SELF-LOVE

Self-love looks to me like no more rage and violent storms within. No more making choices that will crush and smother parts of my soul.

Self-love looks like waking up and feeling complete gratitude for the body I rise in, my heart that beats and my mind that swirls endlessly and quiets itself abruptly.

Self-love gives you permission to feel the doubt, uncertainty and fears, and it arrives with a softness, compassion and a knowing that this too shall pass.

Self-love tucks you in safely at night and awakens you with a gentle kiss.

– Shari Alyse

FOREWORD BY G.O.D.

Let's just talk about the obvious elephant in the room. Yes, this is God. Or G.O.D. as Shari refers (raps) to me. And yes, I've actually been a part of many other books besides the great Book. And let me assure you, this one is great too. I know this because Shari and I have been working on it her entire life. We've been through quite a journey together to get to this point, and no matter what roads we've traversed together, she kept showing up for herself and her life. This is why I knew she had to be the one to share this gift with you.

Shari hasn't always been an easy one to get through to. She has definitely marched to the beat of her own drum which is my loving way of saying I've often had to come up with some creative ways to get her attention. In order to introduce the idea of me being a part of this book, I had to do a little work-around.

As you will come to learn a little later in this book, Shari had quite an affection for Neale Donald Walsch, author of the series, "Conversations with God." Another great work I humbly might add. That was Shari's first conscious awakening to me, so I understand her affection towards him. I spoke to her through him. Now as I mentioned, Shari doesn't always listen the first time around, so I sometimes have to show up in different ways to get her attention.

One day, out of nowhere *(wink),* she decided that Neale should be the one to write the foreword to her book. Now, it's a little challenging to get in touch with Neale and so while she was obsessing about how she would get him to do this, I gently let her know one morning on our walk together that I would be happy to do the writing. I'm not often shocked, but that morning I was. She didn't blink an eye and said, "Okay." I've known Shari her entire life and this is the first time she didn't think 'too' much about it.

Now, when Shari actually sat down to allow me to express myself through her, she worked on giving me a voice that sounded like 'God.' No, not Morgan Freeman. I'm speaking about a writing voice. A lot of therefore's, beloved's, moreover's and thus. Let's just chalk that up to her affection for musicals, movies and plays and basically anything with a dramatic flair. I'll take responsibility for that. I've been known to have a flair for the dramatics now and then.

In truth, I show up for her and you as you know me and understand me. I show up as signs, as songs, as oceans and lovers. To teach you, open you and reflect you. I'm here with you in the joyous moments and especially in the gut-wrenching ones. I am here with you through it all. In this book, I show up as *she* hears me. Someone with a helluva sense of humor mixed with great love. (And humble)

In "Love Yourself Happy", Shari shares her honest journey through this life. Her triumphs and falls. Her walks with darkness and her triumphant climb from its crutches. She travels the world over and looks to everyone and everywhere else to finally come face to face with what has been trying to get her attention all along–her. This story we share with you is the journey towards uncovering *your* light. The journey towards re-discovering your greatest gift–you. You are my greatest work and one that I am so proud of. You are a powerful light in this world, and yet you sometimes forget that and try to smother that light with things that you've come to believe hold more power than you do. The things you run from and try to avoid only to come to find that the answer you've been searching for, the one you have wrestled with and wrestled from has always been you.

So, let's get going! While Shari's trip might not look exactly like yours does, your discoveries are ultimately the same as you all arrive at the same destination. The question only remains: how much love and fun will you have along the way?

Enjoy the journey and remember–I walk alongside of you. I do not choose for you. I step aside and I allow you to find your own way because in that journey you *will* discover all of who you are. And that is the day that I rejoice as you are my greatest masterpiece.

With Great Love,
G.O.D.

P.S. If Shari asks, she doesn't need any more PB&J sandwiches so please gently decline.

CONTENTS

INTRODUCTION

It's a rainy Thursday and I'm working again on just letting these words flow. Not judging them. Not trying to be perfect. But just being me. I think that's been the hardest part of this process for me. Sitting in my ME-ness.

Now that probably doesn't give you much confidence when you're getting ready to dive into a book by someone that is all about self-love. I get it. I'm right there with you. So, I might as well just lay this all out there for you whether you want to hear the truth or not–I DO NOT HAVE THE ANSWERS.

Phew! Literally, my shoulders just dropped. That's why I haven't been able to finish this book. I was speaking with my book coach (yes, coaches have coaches) and we were talking about the blocks that are stopping me from completing this and I simply said that this book carries too much weight. I'm trying to help and save everyone and to carry a burden like that into a book is well, f*cking hard. She looked me dead in the eye and said, "Well that's just not possible, Shari. You can't save the Universe."

What? You mean this isn't going to be the answer for everyone? I'm not going to change millions of lives and everyone's problems aren't going to be solved simply from reading this mind-blowing (just amuse me) book?

Oh. Huh. Okay. Hmmm. (Recalibration here)

So... then I guess I should just write what's in my heart and get my mind and deep need for perfectionism out of the way and get to sharing.

Yup, that's me in a nutshell: the girl with the grand plans, the big dreams, the huge calling–the one that shows up talking about it, shows glimpses of it and then shuts it down. It's not that I don't believe in myself. Hell, I've worked what seems like an eternity on myself to be where I am, but I've still got some baby hairs that need some extra gel to flatten them down. Okay, if we are going to have this relationship, I might as well be completely honest with you from the get-go–I don't really have much hair. I wear a wig.

I wasn't always able to share that so easily. As a matter of fact, I hid it for many years until I realized that it was a lot easier to just tell people and stop trying to be so perfect. Besides, how many awesome hair days can one really have? At some point, somebody was going to figure this shit out.

So, I stepped off my perfect throne and have since told everyone. Including people who don't care to hear, making many uncomfortable and inspiring many others.

That's the thing about self-love. Sometimes you can get so full of it that others can't handle it. And I don't mean full of it like your head is so big you can't fit through a doorway. I mean, you feel so full that sometimes you're unsure how you never, ever saw your light before.

In my defense, it's super hard to see your light when you're carrying around another whole person in you. When you're dragging 270 lbs. on a 5'4" frame. It's hard to see and feel your own light when you're busy dimming it and numbing it with food, men and partying.

Now of course this wasn't on purpose, silly. I was well aware that I was hiding some shit deep down. I wasn't naive enough to think that I just liked Whoppers 'that' much. Nah. I was hiding and protecting me.

Most of us do the same when we hurt. When we've discovered that leaving our hearts and souls wide open leave us vulnerable and that openness and trust is betrayed, shattered, hurt and left scarred. We shut down. I don't blame us. I don't blame you. You're protecting yourself. It's truly where self-love makes its first appearance, although cleverly disguised as fear, mistrust and sadness.

When you and I are kids, we trust the entire world. We trust that we will be taken care of, kept safe and that our open, beautiful and pure hearts will always stay that way. So, we walk into the world shining. Shining so brightly with so much joy that we can't help but feel alive. It's the joy that you recognize in children. It's the reason you light up when you watch them. You see YOU.

But, in this very open place where we allow ourselves to exist and thrive, the adults in our lives have learned at this point to guard themselves. You see, they have sadly experienced hurt, pain and disappointment. So, we begin to feel their 'stuff.' We begin to observe their pain and as children who are sponges, we begin to FEEL their pain. And slowly, over time (and not purposely), they shape us into *their* hurts, *their* mistrust and *their* sometimes bitterness.

It's not their fault. It happened to them, too.

You and I learn that this bright and beautiful place within that felt like freedom in the beginning is no longer safe to remain open. So, we guard. We close off. We shut down. We stop visiting. We begin to seek solace, happiness, fulfillment and contentment (anything that fills this emptiness within) outside ourselves.

3

We seek fulfillment through career, relationships, money, our car, our body, wine, food, STUFF! We turn to it all because there is something missing inside that always feels just not right.

It's YOU! You have separated from YOU. Of course, you're going to feel incomplete. Of course, you're going to feel unfulfilled, unhappy, out of sorts, restless, loveless, anxious, depressed and stressed! You have forgotten and left behind that which makes you whole. YOU.

Wipe those tears up, kid. There's still great news in here!

You are still here.
You haven't gone anywhere.
You have simply been waiting to reunite back with you.

Love Yourself Happy is a journey back to *you*. It's a road trip to self-love. No need to ask anyone for directions (although I'm definitely a backseat driver, so I'll offer some guidance), as you are the *only* one who knows the way back. Thankfully, this takes all the pressure off me to save you (and the Universe) and to simply light up the road so you can see your way back home.

Like any road trip, there will be some unexpected *detours* (challenges), definitely some *rest stops* (lessons learned) and, of course, places to *fuel up* (motivation)!

Enjoy the journey! Hope you're ready for adventure and got some good snacks for the road! I like PB&J (in case you're wondering).

xo
Shari

BACKGROUND

Wait! Pump the breaks! Before we jump on the road and before a total stranger (me) begins dispensing advice to a total stranger (you), I figure you should probably get to know me just a little bit better. The last thing anyone wants to do is hear some mumbo jumbo pretty and inspiring words from someone who hasn't walked through the fire themselves. To be honest, it seems everyone is an expert these days and everyone has the answers to well, everything.

Between you and me, it's B.S.

I am you. I have and am walking through it currently. The journey doesn't end. I have learned amazing lessons in my life, have transformed myself, accepted myself and yes, have fallen in love with myself. But dang, there are hard days! I haven't arrived at the pearly gates of wisdom and ultimate enlightenment. (Has anyone really? If so, tell them I'm looking for them!) I learn lessons and often I discover that there is another deeper one lying just beneath it. But what I learn is so damn beautiful and inspiring and I just can't keep it to myself.

Side Note: While my experiences will look different (because I believe they are tailor made for us so that we understand them), the universal lessons are the same. I am confident that the things I've learned will ring true for others–hopefully for *you*. I know this because someone else's journey helped inspire mine. It lit something up inside me–a truth that I already knew and just needed to be reminded of.

So, as you and I grow our relationship, think of me as your best friend, your co-pilot, your partner in crime who is looking out for you. Some things might resonate for you now and other things you might discover further down the line. Remember the wise words your B.F.F. (that's me!) once said and then smile fondly thinking of me. But until then, I want you to understand where my head was when things started to really fall apart. Spoiler alert: They actually were coming together.

It was 1998 and I was partying too much, hurting too much and then rinsing and repeating too much. I was still suffering over the break-up of my high school sweetheart turned fiancé (in college) and I was trying to fill what felt like gaping holes within, with food, men and parties. But the only thing that got me was more broken hearts, more hangovers and a closet full of size 26 jeans. And I mean the size 26 that comes in plus size at the tippy top of Lane Bryant.

I think I was taught to run. Any time some uncomfortable feeling was wanting to rise to the surface, I shoved it back down. My numbing medication of choice was food. I learned to literally suffocate my feelings with food.

But I wasn't depressed! That's what I would tell myself. Most people around me at that time would tell you that, too—perhaps because they were also drowning their feelings in alcohol and other crutches, but also because I hid it so well, even from myself. The smile plastered on my face, the joyful, always looked happy, always exuberant and filled-with-life Shari. I *really* felt like I was still a pretty happy, 270 lb., 24-year-old. (Shhhh, I hear you muttering to yourself.)

I look back and I see the exact moment in time where my spiritual (re) awakening began. I was sitting in my bedroom in my apartment in Queens, New York in the dark with a few candles lit, my journal next to me. I was immersed in the book *Conversations with God* by Neale Donald Walsh. I'm not sure what I expected to find behind this ink, but what I found changed everything.

It gave me hope.

It settled things within.
It had me breathe just a little easier.
Something ached less.

Of course, I had no idea that this was some awakening, or emerging or even anything 'spiritual'. I just knew that when I did this, I felt better. I knew that when I sat here in this space, feelings right on the surface, emotions sitting on my skin fully exposed, open, being touched in some way – somehow in these moments, I felt just a little bit better.

It wasn't until decades later that I understood what was happening. It wasn't until many bags of chips later that I discovered that what I was doing, what I was experiencing in those quiet moments was the opening of my soul. It was the connecting to it. I was allowing what I was feeling to come out and up to the surface. I was experiencing the re-meeting or reunification with myself.

Me and God.
Me and my soul.
Me and peace.

So why food? Truthfully, it could've been anything–anything that kept me away from feeling. In college, I found myself at the food court in the building next door to my dorm room, drowning my sorrows in Whoppers. In my early 20's in New York City, you could find me late nights on the Upper East Side downing amaretto sours, Goldschlägers and men.

I then decided I had enough of that life and so I moved to Los Angeles where I discovered I liked vodka a lot more than amaretto and men just as much. The truth was, I was dying to find my way, but I just didn't know how. I would find that whenever I got close to connecting within, I jumped ship and drowned myself in something just a little bit more.

Of course, it wasn't obvious to me that this is what I was doing. It came guised in the 'this is what you do in your 20s rationalization. "I'm supposed to have fun and go crazy!" I had no idea I was carrying around this much fear. Again, if you had asked anyone (especially my family), they would've told you that I was so strong and brave (I learned to hate those words), and fear was not in my vocabulary. How many seven-year-olds do you know that get on a witness stand to testify against the old man who touched her inappropriately? Well, this was way before the #TimesUp and #MeToo movement. By the way, thank you for that and for finally feeling like I have a community after 30+ years of speaking out!

So yeah, fear wasn't something I walked around openly feeling. But then again, any feeling I truly had was buried beneath the surface and covered with the mask of love, joy and smiles – what I thought I 'should' feel or be.

You see, for all of us, no matter what traumas we experience, what disappointments, heartbreaks and aches we encounter, no matter how many times we want to run and hide, our souls are just not having it. It's like trying to smother the fire in the sun with a garden hose. It just ain't happening, folks.

So, while you might walk in fear, or sitting on the sidelines of your life, too afraid to move or take a chance, that light burning inside is always reminding you of what you want and what you deserve. It's always whispering to you. Yes, even after you try to quiet it down. Most often it arrives guns ablazing when you ignore those whispers. Usually it shows up as a breakdown, some major catastrophe, health scare or even the end of a career or relationship. When you're not walking down the path that is meant for you, you're always being guided right back to center. When you continue to ignore that guidance, you're pushed back onto that path. It doesn't always feel good, but eventually it will all make sense.

And that is how my journey unfolded. Consistently being shoved back to center because I was the queen of ignoring, stuffing, stifling and distracting. But eventually, we all find our way–every single time. The question isn't whether we do. It's how easy or challenging you want to make your journey and how smooth or obstacle-ridden you want to make that path.

My hope for you is that my story, my journey, will help make your trip a bit easier. I hope that these discoveries and truths will light up the road for you so you feel less alone and so you always know there *is* a way through and ultimately back to beautiful *you*.

> *"The love story I was waiting my entire life for was the greatest love story that's ever been told. It's the one that begins and ends with ME."*
>
> – Shari Alyse

WHAT IS HAPPY IN THE FIRST PLACE?

Who doesn't want to be happy? I mean, every freaking Colgate commercial reminds me that I should be smiling more and looking like I just had the most amazing and life-changing day. But hell! Who can live up to that? Does anyone really feel that way all the time?

I know most of us are waiting for happiness. Waiting for that 'thing' to happen before that elusive happy shows its face. You know what I'm talking about. The 'I'll be happy when' disease. I'll be happy when I lose weight. I'll be happy when I have more money, when I am in a relationship, when my health improves… when, when, when.

If you're like most of society, you've put your happiness on hold for what seems like an eternity because the majority of the time you're so busy trying to achieve those things that by the time you do, you're so freaking exhausted and mentally worn out that you forget that this is even what you wanted in the first place and had convinced yourself that it was the magic elixir to happiness. Now, you've discovered there's actually something *else* you need that will make you happy. Phew!

Sound familiar? Of course, it does! You're reading this book right now in hopes of finding your happy. Gotcha!

Let's chat for a moment about happiness in general. In full transparency, I hate data and statistics but just my word on something may not be enough, so here goes…

In the most recent 'World Happiness Report', only about one third of the population says they are happy. Hooray for the 30% of you! But what about the other 70% of the world? What could be keeping you from being happy? Could it be your weight? Could it be your income, health, relationships, etc.? This line of questioning then leads me to this simple (yet I believe profound) idea I want you to think about: if happiness is based on external circumstances, then it goes to say that if something is *not* happening in your life, then you are *un*-happy. The conclusion here then is that your life would be a constant roller coaster of emotions since things don't always happen as we want them to or if they do, they don't last forever.

Science tells us that things are always shifting, ever-changing. Energy is in constant motion. So, for those who are attaching their happiness to external things, needless to say, you are looking at living a life that might require medication to keep you stable. Now I'm not trying to joke about meds, but I'm simply saying that there has got to be something more constant.

Something more concrete must be the catalyst for sustaining happiness – something that never alters or shifts; something that isn't dependent on things outside of your control: something (or someone) perhaps like *you*.

What if *you* were the constant? What if happiness was possible by one variable and one variable alone–your love for yourself? This means you have at least a 50/50 shot at happiness! This means there aren't a ton of things that could change, go wrong, alter, or disappear. This means, *you* and you alone are in charge of this happiness thing.

Hmmm... not bad odds. Not bad at all.

So, this self-love thing? What does this look like? How does one find it? Discover it? If it was so easy, wouldn't I just be loving the hell out of myself? You'd think, right? Yeah, except since you've separated from yourself for so long, it's kind of hard to just start loving the person you barely know and it's even harder to open yourself back up to the person that once got you hurt in the first place. The open and vulnerable person we once were is the one who got hurt. Allowing that part of ourselves to come back out is challenging.

But here's the thing. If you're about to embark on this road trip back to you, it *is* possible–and there is a grand treasure at the end of your trip. There isn't a risk involved. Love is the payoff. Love is the prize. All you have to do is be *willing* to go on the trip!

So, as mentioned before, I've done a lot of the exploring for you. (You're welcome!) I've even cleared some paths, paved some roads and filled in some potholes. So, enjoy! Be open. Be willing to not always have to know it all. Mostly, be kind to yourself along the way. That's what self-love *really* looks like. (Whoops! I didn't mean to spoil the ending.)

"I am going to look back at my life and be happy how I lived it."

(5/16/2003 journal entry)

13

Detour

THE BREAKDOWN

I don't remember how I ended up on the bottom of my shower floor. I wasn't even sure what had happened and what brought it about. But there I was, crouched in the corner of my shower sobbing uncontrollably. These deep, guttural sounds that I had never heard before were pouring out of me–out of every cell in my body. It seemed almost unhuman. I was trying to catch my breath in between each cry and I just kept swallowing hot water, which made my breathing even more labored. I was trying to get the images out of my head–the way his hands felt, the way I felt, the helplessness, the fear–and yet, each time I tried to block it out, another image or feeling came back.

It was the first time that in thirty years that I had actually re-*lived* it. I had thought about it over the years, but I was never able to fully connect to it. It was almost as if I was always someone watching it rather than living it. But on this day, for a reason I can't explain other than it was time–this day, the memories of Jimmy came back to me.

I was seven years old and I loved and trusted everyone. My parents used to tell me that my sister would hide behind their legs when strangers would come around, but not me. I would walk right up to them, bouncy curls and all, and make them my friend. This day was no different.

I don't really remember too much from that day. The memories are segmented in my head, little moments and pockets in time. It's almost like I hopped around from scene to scene in my mind. That morning, my mom told my sister that I had to tag along with her, her friends and their family to the beach, much to the dismay of my sister, of course. I remember being introduced to Jimmy (who was a "friend" of the family who was watching me) and being left alone with him. He asked me if I wanted a piggyback ride in the sandbar. I don't remember if I was uncomfortable with the idea at first. Seeing as I was never afraid of people, I probably was just fine with it…

… until he started touching me.

Then I remembered that. I remembered all of it. I remembered being asked if I liked it. I remembered being asked if he could put his hand in my swimsuit. I remembered being asked if it felt good. I remembered being afraid of how to answer him. Thinking that if I gave the wrong answer, that he would drown me. I remembered that I called out to my sister a few times to come back and swim and hang out with us, but obviously oblivious to what was happening, she told me that I was fine and to "keep having fun."

I wasn't having fun!

I told the lawyers that. I told the judge that. I told everyone that listened to me that it wasn't fun. I told them all that I was scared, but I just kept letting him do it because I thought he would kill me. I remember being made to feel at fault that I didn't do anything more or say anything. I tried explaining to the defense attorney that he told me that if I told anyone, he would kill my parents. So, all I knew is that I had to be brave. I knew that I had to endure what was hell in order to stay safe and keep my family safe.

I was later praised by my family and loved ones for how strong I was. I was applauded for how brave I was to turn him in and to get on a witness stand and put names to my body parts in front of complete strangers. I was praised for how courageous I had been to tell my story and save other girls from him. They had found out that he had done this to a lot of girls, and so I was lauded as a hero.

I didn't feel like one. I didn't feel brave. I didn't feel strong or courageous. But I was taught that. I was taught that from a young age that I can just bear it and move on. And I had. I told myself my entire life that I had dealt with it. I handled this. I put him in prison. I stood up for myself. I saved other young girls–and I was strong. I was stronger than most – until I wasn't.

Until I found myself that day huddled in a corner of my shower. It was then that I knew that it was time to face what had happened. To not just talk about it but to feel it. To not just throw it under the rug but to shine a spotlight on it for it needed to be seen and really dealt with. I knew that it was time to finally heal this part of me. I knew it was what kept me from healthy relationships. It kept me from respecting myself both with men and my obvious unhealthy relationship with food. It showed up in my overindulgence of alcohol, my occasional nights out with drugs, and my rampant sexual encounters. This morning, I knew that it was time for this to end.

Between you and me, you know what you need to heal. We all do. It all just comes down to whether we are ready to face it or not. Was I? Um, not at that exact moment. I would deal with it later. I had to get to work!

I put on that brave face I had been taught over the years and headed to work, but my tears wouldn't stop. My tears didn't care about bravery. They just wanted out. I couldn't get this feeling out of me. I couldn't shake it. I pulled over to the side of the road, called my boss and just sobbed. I told her I couldn't come into work and I might not be there the next few days. I mumbled something about abuse and memories, and I remember her telling me to take all the time that I need.

I knew I wanted to drive. I had to get out of town. I had to get on an open road and feel no walls around me—just pure openness, uninhibited, free space. I wanted nothing closing in on me. I needed to be with just myself, the road and my thoughts. There is something about that open road. Something that doesn't make me feel trapped in me. It's as if someone has come and unlocked this soul of mine and set it free. This road, any road, leads me to my freedom.

Now, I wasn't sure where I would go, but I just knew I was going somewhere.

Detour

THE MEETING

Seven and a half hours and 107 replays of the same song later, I saw the red rocks in the distance. I had never been to Sedona before, but I've also never been one to pass up blaring signs in my face and when I returned home after the call to my boss, a pop-up ad came across my computer screen for Sedona. So, that's where I went!

I haven't always believed in signs, or rather didn't ever really notice the message within them. But as I got older and started to pay more attention to my life, I began to notice that I was always being guided in some way.

I believe we all are. Yes, you, right now. This book. These words. These signs are everywhere if you just stop long enough to notice them. They aren't always these giant, blinking billboards telling you what to do or which direction to go, but they are often a bit more subtle. It could be lyrics to a song you're supposed to hear that day. It could be a book that somebody speaks about that touches you in an unexpected way. It could be a bumper sticker on a car in front of you that somehow is exactly what you're supposed to read. Signs show up in different ways for different people, but they are tailor-made exactly for you so that you pay attention. Now, whether you choose to follow these signs and listen to that guidance is a completely different story.

This day, however, there was no choice—at least not on my part. I hadn't chosen this place. IT had chosen ME.

The main thing I knew about Sedona was that people were healed there. I had heard there were some crazy, intense energies that existed within the vortexes of these mountains. To be honest, I didn't know what the hell that meant. I just knew that I had always wanted to go somewhere that people called "spiritual" and this was deemed the most "spiritual" place in the United States. So, there I was, headed east towards some crazy rocks. It made no sense and yet, it made all the sense in the world.

I got to my motel and turned in early because tomorrow was the big day! The day that would change everything! I know—nothing like having no expectations. And trust me, I was trying to not have expectations. The only time I find myself disappointed in life is when I expect a certain outcome, so I did what anyone who was trying to *not* have expectations would do. I fooled myself into thinking that I didn't have any. I told myself, "I am open to whatever happens even if it is nothing but just a fun time." But, for God's sake, let's be honest. I was driving five hundred miles for *something* to happen. Anything. Mainly, I just needed these tears to stop.

Upon sunrise, I gathered all my stuff, checked out and headed out to the vortexes. After some 'interesting' and still to this day unexplainable and unreal moments, I realized it was time to go home. I don't know what I was expecting, but it wasn't what I came looking for. But in my usual optimistic way, I found the good and the meaning in the visit and I started heading out of town.

Hold up! Not so fast there, Sparky. Are you kidding me? I don't freaking give up! For f' sake, I got led here! Something, *anything* more than getting lost for five hours and finding myself teetering on the edge of a cliff had to be here waiting for me. I'm not done! But where? I researched every vortex and their meanings, and the only thing left that was on my way out of town was the Airport Mesa vortex, so I stopped there.

I had reached the top of this vortex and was ready to go back to my car because, again, nothing! I turned the corner to take one final look at the vista and there she was. Now that might sound dramatic and it should, because there she was. Or should I say there *I* was. No big hoopla. Just my 7-year-old self sporting that awkward tomboy looking stage, 70's hair, blue shorts with the white stripe down the sides, my camp t-shirt and my white knee-high athletic socks with matching double blue stripes at the top.

There I was.

Just sitting there. Back leaning up against a rock, knees tucked close to my chest with my arms wrapped around them. I looked at her, she (me) looked up at me and spoke to me as if we had talked all the time and said all sassy-like, "Took you long enough." (Yup, that was definitely me.)

Now, I know this sounds crazy. I know this! I'm well aware, but as much as I *know* it sounds crazy, I equally *know* that it happened. I *know* that I sat down next to her and spoke for what seemed like an eternity, but probably was more like a few minutes as we were interrupted by a giggling young couple (who certainly weren't looking for spiritual healing at the airport vortex). I *know* that we both cried. I *know* that I made promises to her. I *know* I told her that I had to start looking out for me and taking better care of myself.

And then, I walked away from her. I left her there. I couldn't look back. Truthfully, I didn't want to. I didn't want to know if she wasn't there. I didn't want to know if *somehow* I had imagined it. I *knew* I hadn't, but

I didn't want to take any chances. I just knew that I found what I was looking for and it was time to go home. It was time to let that part of my life go and to start a new chapter. It was time to start living.

I played the same song on repeat the entire drive home. I turned up the volume on that baby and sang my heart out. Only this time, there was a sense of sadness or darkness. I can't really explain it, but it was like there was something I knew I was missing or leaving behind. Maybe it was fear that that moment I had, that trip I took wouldn't solve it all. I am not sure where I learned this from–this idea that there is a pretty red bow that comes wrapped around that thing you've been working on with a big ol' black stamp that says, 'SOLVED!'

That's what I assumed I was doing with that moment on that mountaintop. I am certain I knew how big it was, but my hopes were to write about it and then tuck it away with lesson and wisdom learned and move on. But this feeling… this heavy feeling would not escape me on this drive home. No matter how loud I played that song, I couldn't drown out this feeling that something just wasn't right.

I returned home and went back to life. Returned the next night to serve steaks and fries, thanked my manager for giving me that time and held those days in Sedona in the back of my mind. I didn't share that with anyone yet. I wanted to keep it for me. They were my moments, my healing, and my time.

About a week went by and I shared my experience with my mom. I had to say the words aloud, I had to make sense of them. Of course, there was no making sense of this moment. The beautiful thing was that my mom, who I know didn't really understand this but always supported me, just listened. She stayed quiet while I went on and on about what I thought it meant, how it would change me, what I was wearing, how crazy it sounded and whatever else I rambled on about. She listened.

Then she simply said, "God sent her to you, Shari. It's now time to let all of this go."

I knew she was right, but I still had this damn nagging feeling that this wasn't it and she wasn't gone. There was something that I was still missing. Some puzzle piece that was out of place and I hadn't quite figured out where. Why couldn't I ever just leave well enough alone? I mean, I had an experience that most don't ever imagine having and here I was still wanting more. But that's how I've always been. Always seeking. Always watching. Always discovering. Always wanting more.

But for now, I was tucking this away in the bottom drawer. I was done looking at it.

Rest Stop 1

FACE YOUR SH*T

*"Every challenge you face in your life is there
for you and divinely guided to you."*

– Shari Alyse

I'm sure you've read this quote on a zillion inspirational memes or one of your super positive friends told you this during some hurt you were experiencing (annoying). Believe me, I was *not* wanting to see how my ex-fiancé's philandering ways were 'good for me in the long run'! I certainly wasn't fond of the idea that this was 'divinely' guided to me! I mean, what kind of God would want me to suffer and feel that kind of brokenness?

I get it.
I hear you.

And the only thing I can say to you is this and you're probably not going to like it if you're currently going through something crappy.

(Whispers) "It is *for* you."
(Sorry, I'm one of those super positive and annoying people, too.)

And although I know this is absolutely true, I also get how hard it is to see that right now in the midst of a crappy situation. But the reality is, every single difficult thing that I've been through has worked out for me. Now, I didn't always see it clearly at the time because I was too busy trying to outrun it. I was too busy trying to push it away or curse it because I didn't want to face what it was trying to show me and whatever message "gift" it was trying to give to me. Screw that, I've been hurt enough. I'm certainly not going to purposely uncover more pain.

"What is meant for you to heal will always find its way."

– Shari Alyse

The part of you that needs to heal will show up in different ways. It can be that incessant whisper that is always reminding you that there's 'more for you', or that lover who keeps showing up in your life disguised as different people breaking your heart again and again trying to get you to heal something within, or it's chronic health issues demanding to get your attention. They always show up again.

But I get it. It seems much easier to stuff down anything that doesn't feel comfortable. I understand that when things rise to the surface, it brings up stuff that you don't want to experience again. It feels easier to just not deal with it. But here's the thing–the more you stuff down what you're truly feeling, the more that bubbles just below the surface and ultimately will erupt at some point.

You are a container. You can only hold so much before it begins to affect you emotionally, physically and mentally. So, while the idea of keeping your real feelings at bay sounds like a brilliant idea, the truth of the matter is that in the facing and dealing with it in that moment, it ends up being much more of a tremor than the impending, often devastating internal earthquake that can occur.

The good news is (thank God!), no matter if it's a tremor or that earthquake, you'll make it through. I made it through. We all do. It's not really a question of *if* you will get through it, but rather *how* you want to move through it.

For many years, I went kicking and screaming through life. The constant pity parties, questions and woeful declarations of "Why is this happening to *me*? Why am *I* being punished? I'm a good person! I don't deserve this!" I have since come to skip that part because it causes nothing but prolonged suffering. No matter how hurt I was, what circumstance knocked me to my knees, I *always* discovered the lesson and yes, even the blessing in it.

So, ol' Sherlock Holmes here began to finally catch on to this pattern and realized that first, it was much easier when these things popped up to just face them. I needed to face my shit because I certainly wasn't going to outrun it. Secondly, I needed to trust in what was happening because, ultimately, I would discover that it wasn't here to sever me, but rather serve me. Now when these challenging moments arise, I no longer ask, "Why me?" I ask instead, "What have you come to show me?"

Here's the thing, my beautiful friend (can I call you that?), you were built and are made of stars. You hold a magic and a power and light that no person or circumstance can burn out. So, while you believe that you can't handle one more thing, let me assure you that there is nothing that can shake you once you know who you really are and what you really can do.

Perhaps you might be thinking, "I can't go through this one more time, Shari. I sometimes feel like I can't even breathe." Once you begin to understand your strength, you will stop experiencing these situations to the extent and magnitude that you once did. They will no longer suffocate and drown you. They will be minor disturbances in the bigger picture of your life. You will come to understand that they have in fact *all* been divinely placed there for you so that you can ultimately see and know *your* power. When you go from the mindset of victimhood to victor, you will stop seeing life as though it's punishing and devouring you. You will open your eyes to the lessons, the teachers and the hidden messages of love underneath it all.

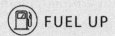 **FUEL UP**

On the road to self-love, stop running. Muster up the courage to turn around and face what is simply trying to get your attention so you can heal it. And most importantly (as you will come to find out later), it's only asking for your attention because it's simply wanting you to love those parts of you that you've forgotten to love. And as a super cool bonus, you will come to find out that you are always being guided back to love. To you. Everything that happens and everyone you meet are guides to lead you there. So, don't forget your angel radar! You'd be shocked, they are everywhere.

Psst—go easy on yourself.

Rest Stop 2

SUNDAE TOPPED
WITH GUILT

Like clockwork, every Friday night the horn would honk outside of our house and my sister and I would grab our weekend bags, say goodbye to our mom and hop in the car with our dad for a fun-filled weekend! And just like clockwork, the guilt of leaving one parent for another set in. Was my mom mad? Was she going to be okay alone? We were off to go have fun and she was stuck with nothing to do. Was she upset that we had fun with him?

Then just like clockwork, dad would drop us off on Sunday night and the guilt of leaving him to go back home set in. Was he mad that he just spent an entire weekend entertaining us and now we were leaving him? Would *he* be okay? Was he mad that he only saw us twice a month? Did he think we didn't want to see him? I mean, I couldn't escape for a moment this guilt that felt like a cement block attached at my ankle that I was dragging around everywhere.

GUILT.

I'm not sure if it's because I was born into a Jewish family and we bleed guilt in every word, every sigh, every 'oy vey', or if it's something else, but man oh man, I'm certain that guilt is responsible for at least 50 lbs. on my body. Or at least for these thighs. Guilt for loving a parent that made some big mistakes, guilt for wanting everyone to be happy, guilt for having compassion for someone somebody else doesn't like, guilt for forgiving someone that someone else hasn't forgiven. I mean, guilt just has steered my ship for many years.

I'm not saying that it was my family's fault. Ultimately, we are responsible for our own feelings. But I do have to say, however, that when you're surrounded by guilt, it's kind of hard to not allow that to effect who you are and how you walk through the world.

Perhaps it's not guilt for you. Maybe it's some other something that feels like quicksand and like you're dragging a dead body around. Whatever that 'something' is for you, the road to self-love comes with the realization that you don't have to carry *any* of this around. You and I hold the key to releasing anything that is literally weighing us down!

Now you might be thinking, *how?* The most important thing is the recognition that you've been dragging some lifeless, unimportant, not yours, dead body around with you. Once you can *see* that, then you're able to decide if you want to stay attached to it. The real problem is that so many of us don't even realize that we've been lugging these things around. We don't know that we carry guilt, anger, disappointment, etc. on our shoulders. We are so used to carrying it that it feels like it's just part of our load. But once you see it and understand that you no longer need to carry it, then it becomes a lot easier to cut that shit off!

🅿 FUEL UP

On the road to self-love, take a pause and a good look at what you have tied around your ankles. What have you been dragging through this life that might not be yours to carry? Then be willing to hand it back. To simply declare, "I love you, but this is **not** my burden to carry. I hand it back to you with love and allow you to take responsibility with it as you see fit. For me, I am loving myself back to happy and this ain't part of my outfit anymore!"

Psst–go easy on yourself.

Rest Stop 3

YOUR FEELINGS ARE NOT WRONG

"You shouldn't feel that way."
"You're crazy!"
"That's your problem!"

I can't recall how many times someone has said that or something like that to me because truthfully, there were too many times. People told me that what I was feeling was wrong or what I was feeling was not justified. They told me these things so many times that I started thinking perhaps there was something wrong with me. Maybe I was too much? Maybe I needed to close off my heart and not feel or care so much? This then turned into me thinking that I needed to play a certain role in these relationships so I wouldn't come off crazy to them. I then began acting aloof and pretending that I wasn't looking for a serious relationship and only wanted a casual one, which then of course led me to getting my heart broken time and time again because that was all that I was getting from them.

Sound familiar? Have you been told these things before or made to feel that your feelings are wrong? I call this the 'super-master-manipulative-take-responsibility-off-myself' response to you expressing your feelings to someone. Basically, this is my term for someone who doesn't want to hold any responsibility for their actions and so they blame you for how you're feeling. (i.e. too sensitive, too emotional, too needy, too attached, too dependent, etc.)

For many years, I felt embarrassed about being sensitive. I felt there was something wrong with me because I loved so much, and I felt dumb for getting so hurt in relationships. And here's the question: was I too sensitive sometimes? Maybe. Did I love to the extreme (not in a creepy, stalker way) sometimes? Yeah, perhaps. But in every situation, my feelings were valid and should've been taken in with love, compassion and understanding.

When I first started dating my current fiancé, he had been betrayed in a very bad way, so he came into our relationship with understandable fears, worries and insecurities. I believed it was my job (because I cared for him) to make sure that he didn't have to have these doubts and fears. It was not my job to make him feel badly about what he rightfully was feeling. Sure, I am not the one that betrayed him; however, I am human, and I understand what betrayal feels like and I would do everything in my power to not make him feel that way.

That is when I truly understood what loving someone really looked like. It never was a burden to make him feel safe in our relationship. It never was a burden to call him when I went somewhere to tell him where I was. He never asked for it, but I wanted to give him that because I loved him.

If you are feeling insecure in a relationship, whether romantic or platonic, the person in that relationship with you, if they truly care about you, will sit with you and do what they can to help ease your mind. They will help make you feel more secure. They will help you through this. They will not make you feel badly or guilty or like there is something wrong with you.

For God's sake, we all have been through some shit and we all have been hurt, and wouldn't you want someone to be patient with you and love you through it and sit with you through it? So, why the hell would I not give that to someone else? And that is what *you* deserve, too.

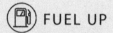 FUEL UP

On the road to self-love, make sure that you are sitting in a place with someone who loves you enough and cares enough about you to hold your hand when you're going through some shit. Make sure it is someone who validates your feelings and allows you to feel them without guilt and shame. You are deserving of loving yourself full and surrounding yourself with those who will help you do that, too.

Your feelings are valid and so are you.

Psst—go easy on yourself.

Rest Stop 4

STOP TRYING TO LOOK ON THE BRIGHT SIDE!

Um, excuse me? I know, I know, but pick up your jaw and please hear me out. I know this goes against everything you've ever been taught, from your mom, to your best friend to hell, even bumper stickers and T-shirts. This is probably the single best and worst advice ever, or it at least needs to come with a disclaimer. Yes! Please look on the bright side of a shitty situation. But please, also be willing to not ignore *why* this is happening.

Saying positive things and thinking positive things absolutely helps you in those moments, but we also often use it to ignore the underlying issue. There is something deeper that is creating those negative feelings. There is something deeper that is calling you to listen to what the hell it's trying to say. And it's your job to not put icing on it, but rather to dig into it and figure out the real reasons why things keep showing up the way that they do, why people keep treating you the same way or why you keep ending up broke every month.

Positive affirmations are amazing. They got me through some really crappy moments in my life and they allowed me to keep my head above water. Knowing that "everything happens for a reason" helped me deal better with the breakups, the disappointments and breakdowns. It kept me (somewhat) sane as I tried to make sense of things. As I tried to figure out *how* this could be happening again to me. But here's where the real breakdown in 'looking at the bright side' (or any other positive, shiny affirmation) comes in–when you start making excuses for people. Things break down when you continue to make choices that don't align with your truth and you just believe that it will "always work itself out."

Yes, while it's true that everything will work out, the journey there doesn't have to be filled with pain, extra obstacles and with suffering. When we look at a situation for what it *really* is and allow ourselves to ask the right questions and not positively affirm our feelings away, then you gift yourself with the room to grow and expand. Continually shoving chips in your mouth while stating that "*all is well*" really is contradicting itself. If all was well, we wouldn't have to resort to food (or drugs, vodka, shopping, etc.) to numb ourselves.

So, all these self-help gurus and all these people who promise you that life is easy if you just 'change your thoughts', while they are partially correct, there is another part of this that you must be willing to deal with. And it's not always an easy job, but truth be told, it also wasn't easy for you to get to this point.

 FUEL UP

On the road to self-love, when moments of heartbreak or heartache sneak up on you and leave you short of breath, look on the bright side and allow yourself to be comforted by words of love and hope, and also remember to gift yourself by honoring what is showing up in terms of real feelings. Give them a voice. Don't just pat them on the head and hush them up with a few sweet words. Your soul will thank you for it.

And always remember, "After every storm, there is a rainbow."

(I joke, I joke!)

Psst—go easy on yourself.

Rest Stop 5

CHOOSE YOU

She answered the phone half asleep. With what felt like a 100 lb. weight sitting on my chest and through trembling voice and racing heart, I asked if I could speak to Mike*. She said hold on, and he quickly said, "Hello." I didn't need to hear another word. I didn't need to ask any questions. I knew he was lying next to her. But I somehow squeezed out the word "hello" and all I heard on the other side was a big exhale.

That was the moment.

That was when I knew my heart would never be the same. That was the moment I felt like I just might never trust or love again. I didn't expect it. I mean, it came out of left field. I thought I was his everything. Never doubted it. No matter that we currently were on a break. I thought it was because we just needed to figure ourselves out. I had gone off to college and he was back in our hometown trying to figure out life without me. But I didn't realize he was trying to replace me or at least that's what it felt like.

That is where I believe my journey of feeling easily dispensable, unimportant and abandoned began. It was in this moment.

I gave up secure relationships.

I gave up comfort.

I chose unavailable, risky and safe. (And by safe, I mean I knew we couldn't be together.)

I chose to be the driver so I wouldn't be surprised where we ended up.

And I chose heartbreak after heartbreak.

You see, no matter how much I convinced myself that I didn't want a relationship and just wanted a no-strings attached good time, I always secretly (mostly to myself) hoped that they would fall in love with me and *choose* me and that I would be it! I would be the one that made them change their bachelor or promiscuous ways. I hoped that I would be the one that made them leave their life, their wife (yes, sadly), their anything. I just wanted to feel that I was *enough*. But that didn't happen. I was exactly to them what I had put out there to them and how I had showed up for myself—as a side note.

People will never see what we want them to see until we start being the person we are trying to be. It wasn't until I began being truthful with myself about who I was and what I wanted that it began to show up.

And I'm talking about being brutally honest with yourself. I'm not talking about what you think you should feel or say. I'm talking about being honest with your deep, burning, no-holds bar truth—the part that aches within you and speaks to you in silence at night when you lay your head down. I'm talking about that voice, that truth, that *you*.

When I allowed this part of myself to speak up, love found me. I began to see me. This is when I finally exhaled—deeply.

FUEL UP

On the road to self-love, make sure that you choose you–without question. Put your needs before someone else's. When you do this, you are creating a healthy and well-balanced you. You then show up for someone else even better. You will be less selfish because you will not be needing anything from them. You will show up for the world ready to share and not take. You will show up in your life feeling content and loved. You won't feel the need to step on or step over with your expectations and conditions. You will see that you are just you. Beautiful and whole you.

Choose you–every single time.

*Names have been changed to protect the guilty

Psst–go easy on yourself.

Rest Stop 6

LEARN TO SPEND TIME WITH YOU

I used to have to be around people all the time. If it wasn't actual humans, it was music, television, books–anything but around my own thoughts and my own self. Of course I hadn't self-analyzed myself just yet, but what I did know was that every time I tried to go quiet within, every time I was just at the precipice of touching something deeper inside of me, of finding that stillness within, I ran for the hills! I literally felt myself leap out from that space within. This didn't happen just during meditation. I had to be busy and distracted all the time. I was always going out and always involved in something and with something. It's as if I was afraid to sit with *me*.

And I know I'm not alone. I know this might be you, too. Perhaps you're afraid to get quiet. Maybe you don't want to look at the deeper stuff. Maybe by going quiet, the uncomfortable things pop up. But as mentioned in 'Face Your Sh*t', you can't outrun it, so you might as well start getting to know yourself. No matter how much you try to avoid spending time with yourself, you will always be there. Louise Hay once said, "The longest relationship you will ever have is with yourself, so you might as well make it a good one."

So, I learned to take myself out on dates. After the devastating breakup with my high school sweetheart, I made a vow to be single. Well, that's the romanticized version I told myself. The truth was, I first tried to distract myself with other men, booze and food; but once that didn't work, once I woke up after each hangover, with each stranger and with added weight, *I* was still there. What I was trying to run from and avoid (me), still lingered there. At some point, I had to face the fact that I wasn't going anywhere. I decided it was time to put my big girl undies on and start learning to like the reflection that was staring back at me every day. I certainly wasn't going anywhere, and neither are you, my beautiful friend.

I began taking myself to movies. I went out for nice dinners. I took long walks, read great books and even traveled alone. I started spending so much time with myself that I began to look forward to that special time with me. I found myself making excuses to *not* hang out with people.

Now don't go becoming a recluse (I did that, too) but do learn to appreciate and relish the time with you. One of the greatest things about spending time alone with yourself is that you always get to see the movie *you* want to see. When you're bored, *you* can leave. You don't have to share the bread on the table and you certainly don't have to laugh at jokes that aren't funny (that's exhausting). You get to tell the corniest jokes and laugh at them!

⛽ FUEL UP

On the road to self-love, take some time getting to know you. Court yourself. Treat yourself to things that fill your soul and lift your spirit. You're with you for the long haul, so make your relationship with you like a fairy tale! (If you're into that sort of thing.)

Psst—go easy on yourself.

Rest Stop 7

SOMETIMES, SH*T JUST SUCKS!

Getting cheated on? SUCKS! Your car breaking down when you are completely broke? SUCKS! Tearing the ligaments in your knee right before a possibly life-changing audition? SUCKS! Do you hear me?! SUCKS!!!

I don't care how you look at it–sometimes shit does just suck. No matter how you package it, what pretty bow you decorate it with, sometimes you have to bawl your damn eyes out, punch a pillow, curse at somebody (please try not to do this) and then call it a mother-freaking day.

I'm the queen of finding the positive and gift in everything *(see previous chapter, 'Stop Trying to Look on the Bright Side!')* and that gets exhausting. More so than that, it can also make you or the person that is in pain feel like you're diminishing theirs or your own feelings. Let me explain.

I always wanted to fix everything for everyone. I know that it feels better to feel better and so I learned from an early age how to mask the bad feelings I was feeling. I covered them with positive platitudes and learned how to make others feel better with them, too. But that doesn't always work. I have been told on more than one occasion, "Sometimes, Shari, I just want to be heard and I don't need a solution." What? Who doesn't want a solution? Why the hell would you not want to feel better? I thought it was just someone who wanted to complain and sit in their misery. And while there are people like this, the truth is, sitting *in* your feelings *is* okay. Not having to find a solution for them *is* okay. Sometimes, there isn't a solution. Sometimes, shit does just SUCK. And there are times that it absolutely calls to throw your hands in the air and say, "F it! This sucks!" And if you're in this place right now, I encourage you to do it! Yell at the top of your lungs!

Here's the great thing about accepting that not everything is always going to be great. Once I was able to accept that some things just don't feel good or go my way, the journey through my life became much easier. I stopped trying to make sense of it and find the deeper meaning in it, and yes, even stopped suffering through it. I was able to walk out the other side much more quickly because I just accepted that shitty things happen sometimes and the only thing you and I can keep doing is just keep moving. Just keep showing up for life, showing up for others and showing up for ourselves.

So yes, while you may be a seeker of deeper wisdom and insight (like myself), every now and again, life calls for you to just give it up and hand it over. Ahhhh, breathe through that. Say it aloud with me, *"Sometimes shit does just suck!"*

⛽ FUEL UP

On the road to self-love, no matter how much you wish for differ-ent circumstances, there are just some things that are out of your control and you're just going to have to throw your arms up in the air and take the suck that comes with it. It's all okay. It will be okay. You are okay.

Phew–now that we've gotten that out of the way, go be awesome!

Psst–go easy on yourself.

Rest Stop 8

NOT EVERYONE IS GOING TO LIKE YOU

I spent many years saying *"yes"* to people. I wanted so desperately to be liked. I didn't want people to think that I wasn't a nice person. So, I was often agreeable. I didn't want to rock the boat because if I did, that might alter your perception of my niceness. I spent so much time catering to others needs that I lost myself along the way. I worried so much about *your* needs, that I gave up my own along the way. And then I shockingly wondered why I was feeling taken advantage of, not appreciated and unseen. The reality was that I wasn't expressing my truth; then I got mad at you because you didn't see the real me.

Truth be told, part of the reason I did that was because I didn't know what it was that I wanted or even liked. I didn't know who I really was. I literally had to travel halfway around the globe and go to a country where I didn't know the language and spend time alone to figure me out. (I'll take you on that trip later!) And finally, in that figuring out of me, I came to this conclusion:

Not everyone is going to like you.
"What you talkin' bout, Willis?"

Seriously? I gave up my truth. I showed up as you wanted me to. Hell, I became a vegetarian for almost a year and the entire time all I wanted was a Big Mac! No matter how I molded myself, at the end of the day, it just wasn't enough. So, finding peace in this place of knowing that I wasn't going to always be liked gifted me the freedom to show up as me–the girl who liked two all-beef patties with special sauce on a sesame seed bun, the girl who hated talking about politics, who cried in commercials, who looked in mirrors when she cried pretending she was in a movie and who ultimately just wanted to be loved. Yes, that was me in all my imperfect glory. And hell, I finally showed up as her! And guess what? People liked me! And... they didn't. And both were okay.

Now some of you might be thinking, "I don't give a damn who likes me." Well, I beg to differ. I believe we all care. And those who say they don't care simply say that to protect themselves from being hurt. The truth is, we all want to affect others in some way. We all want to have made an impact on someone, had meaning in this world and to be appreciated and loved. Otherwise, why would we be here on this Earth if not to connect and commune with others. So, this idea that you shouldn't care at all, I'm not sure if that's really being honest with ourselves.

And before you get cracking on me, I'm not saying (for those of you who are rolling your eyes and getting your defense statement ready) that you live your life and make choices based on what others think. I am saying, however, that most of us do try to show up and be good people, do the right thing and make a good impression in some way because we DO care what people think. And that is not a bad thing. It's when you sacrifice who you really are and what you really want in order to hopefully make people like you.

And here is the big kicker–even if you do know yourself and present your best self, you come to find out that no matter how much you do, there are certain people who just won't like you. It could be your boss that you're trying so hard to impress, or someone you're dating and pretending to love discussing politics while you secretly want to stab yourself in the eye. If you spend your life trying to seek approval from others and not being who you really are in the process, then even if the world falls hopelessly in love with you and everyone thinks you're the best, *you* will still be unhappy. Ultimately, who they love is not who you really are and who you find yourself pretending to be, you won't love either.

Everyone loses when we are not living in our authenticity.

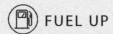 FUEL UP

On the road to self-love, the greatest thing you can ever do is simply be you -not some dimmed and dumbed down version of you, but all of you. Flawed you! Imperfect you! Magnificent you! And when you can do this, you will feel so damn good in your own skin that if someone doesn't like you, you simply won't pay them any mind. You know that the best part of your day is waking up as you. These people will simply be background noise in your life that you are able to fade out.

Psst—go easy on yourself.

Rest Stop 9

JOY DOESN'T DISCRIMINATE

In 2010 I was sitting on an airplane on my way to Haiti with a volunteer group a few weeks after their devastating earthquake. I was sitting there thinking about all the love and help we were going to bring them. I was riding high on all the ways we were going to help these grief-stricken people. I remember thinking beyond all the supplies, probably what they most needed was love, some hugs and a big smile. They needed people there to give them hope, to lift their spirits and bring some joy. I was set and ready for this!

STOP THE PRESS! Hold on there, tiger.

I showed up to the most desolate and poor of places. Destruction everywhere. Homes with missing roofs, children with missing limbs, parents with missing kids. But the one thing that they weren't missing was joy.

I arrived at a children's orphanage expecting devastation and what I witnessed was like nothing I had ever experienced. I saw the biggest smiles I had ever seen. I saw love and I felt their hope. In the midst of having lost it all, there was this palpable joy that I couldn't explain. It didn't make sense in my mind, but my heart knew. My soul knew that they knew a secret that most of us don't.

Joy isn't dependent on what you have, what you do or who you are.

We are joy. We carry it and nobody and no-thing can ever take that away from us. Joy is our birthright and no matter what circumstances show up in our lives, we get to choose to live in it and lead *with* it.

I remember it was a Sunday when we all gathered under their big oak tree with all the children, the workers and volunteers while they held a makeshift church ceremony. Children were laid out on the grass in wooden stretchers or in wheelchairs. Parents held their infants in bandages. Each one of them sang their hearts out! Huge smiles were on their faces and yes, tears in their eyes and a whole lot of joy in their hearts. I had (and still haven't) ever seen or felt anything like that. It was the first time I truly understood what joy was. Joy reminds me of our ticklish spots. It's always there lying right below the surface just waiting to be awakened.

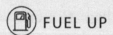 **FUEL UP**

On the road to self-love, when you give yourself permission to be here right now and feel this moment, there is a palpable joy that lifts from your soul. And it's not always obvious. It doesn't always lead the way. But it's there. And the thing that I've learned is that part of loving yourself is gifting yourself permission to feel this joy. Go ahead—tickle it!

Psst—go easy on yourself.

Rest Stop 10

I AM RIGHT– HEAR ME ROAR

My friends (and ex's) knew me as the girl who had to always have the last word. Every argument, *I* had to be the one to end it. I had to get my point across. And honestly, I never knew that I was this way. I just knew that I had a lot to say and I believed strongly in what it was that I was saying. But, over the years, having heard more than one person mention this to me, I have done some self-reflection and have since come to understand that I was (and still sometimes am) fighting for my voice to be heard.

I wanted to be seen and not swept or brushed aside. In my very vocal defense of what we were speaking about, my retorts never really had anything to do with proving the subject at hand, but rather everything to do with not wanting to feel ignored. It wasn't until very recently that I understood what I was doing and more importantly, where this really was stemming from.

As a seven-year-old girl who called out for help and wasn't heard, I have spent years making sure that my voice is now heard. It's the reason I get on stages; it's the reason I have to have the last word; and it's also the reason I have such a tough time listening and spend more of it yapping. (God, I have good friends.)

In this fighting to be right, I've ended up defending myself and arguing with others simply because of how I wanted to feel. I have since discovered that being right doesn't always equate to being happy. And in my life now and on this journey, I'd rather be a whole lot of happy then a whole lot of right. (Thank you, Wayne Dyer!)

At some point, you must stop defending yourself. Sometimes you have to recognize when you don't have to hold on anymore to your beliefs. I don't mean beliefs in the things that you feel deeply about; I mean beliefs where you always feel like you *must* be right. I have defended myself to the ends of the world just to be right. And what I have come to find is that in this fighting to be right, I've lost friends along the way and ended up alone. But hey, at least I was right! And alone.

That was a tough one to learn about myself.

 FUEL UP

On the road to self-love, some of the things you will discover about yourself may not be the prettiest things you had hoped to uncover. However, do not beat yourself up over them. The things you will encounter on this road are all there to direct and guide you and to remind you that we are often imperfect. Actually, we are always imperfect. So, the expectations that you won't do anything wrong , that everybody will like you or that you're always right is simply a theory that you must let go. And in this letting go, freedom will be your reward.

Psst–go easy on yourself.

Rest Stop 11

THEY SCREWED UP!

"Your daughter is very intelligent, but she is a motor mouth." "Slow down, the words aren't going anywhere." "Take a breath, Shari." Or the worst, "You have such a beautiful face if only you'd lose weight."

Ahhhh! I didn't realize that I spent most of my life trying to show up and be what everyone needed me to be. I spent most of my life trying to say the right things, to not rock the boat, to choose the right side and to fit into the box that made everyone else feel okay about themselves.

I love and adore my parents more than anything, but I'm just going to put this out there. They screwed up! My grandparents, they screwed up! My teachers, they screwed up, too!

And I bet yours did, too!

Now, I'm not here to blame anyone else because ultimately you and I are responsible for how we walk through the world, how we show up in our relationships and how we show up for ourselves. I am going to just lay this out there–the people in your life who raised you and had influence over you screwed up. They made mistakes. They did their best, but their own personal beliefs about themselves and the world around them guided them in teaching you limited ways of thinking and being. You see, most likely, they were taught that in order to feel worthy and receive love or be accepted, there were certain things they had to do in order to prove themselves worthy of this love.

It's bullshit.

Everything you and I have been taught and most likely spent our lives jumping through hoops trying to be noticed, and loved, and good enough, is and was a complete waste of time.

You, from the moment you took your first breath were good enough.

I'm going to repeat that in case you need to hear it again–*you*, from the moment you took your first breath and until the moment you take your last–are good enough.

Exhale. Cry if you need to.

There is nothing you need to prove, no dance you have to dance, nothing you must do or achieve in order to have value in this world. I know this might be hard to take in. I spent most of my life performing on world stages, trying so hard to be seen, noticed, appreciated and valued, while searching for my worth through my accomplishments, relationships, body image, talent and service-oriented work. We do all this work to believe that our lives and ourselves have meaning and worth.

Making us feel like we need to prove our worth was a simple mistake on the parts of those who loved us because they hadn't figured out how to love themselves. It's not your fault. But I'm here to tell you that no matter how much you do, or how much you accomplish or how brightly you show up in the world, your worth here has no conditions and can't ever be taken away. It simply can't.

There is love that sits in the spaces in between your breath, that exists in every moment and in everything that is *yours*. You will always receive that which has always been yours. Of course, I didn't always know this. I have searched the world over for love. I have stepped forward and I have retreated. I have given over and I have given up. I have flashed this smile and all my goods, and I have hidden away to take a break from it all. No matter what I've done and how I've chosen to show up or not show up, my worth, value and beauty have never once altered—only my beliefs about them.

But like one's belief in the roundness or flatness of the Earth, what one believes simply does not make it true. Our beliefs can disillusion us and misguide us. I am here to share with you that you are everything you were created to be and there is nothing you need to do right now to make that so.

I invite you to sit with that. Choose that truth over any other one. Take your rightful seat on your throne and settle into the immense beauty that is *you*.

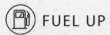 FUEL UP

On the road to self-love, remember, nobody else and no-thing you do or don't do will ever change your enough-ness. Take a deep look into your eyes today and say, "You are enough, and I love you just as you are."

And remember, they screwed up, but you don't have to any longer.

P.S. This 'motor mouth' of mine now goes around the world speaking and uses her voice to inspire thousands. Take that, Mrs. Felkowski!

Psst—go easy on yourself.

Rest Stop 12

SPEAK UP (EVEN IF YOUR VOICE IS TREMBLING)

I was seven years old and I didn't understand too much about any of this except what had happened to me wasn't the norm. Most second grade girls don't have to go to criminal court and testify on a witness stand naming aloud parts of their body to a room full of strangers and to the old man sitting across from her who happened to be the one who touched her inappropriately. Most young girls don't have to defend themselves to a room full of adults trying to explain why she didn't do more to get out of this situation.

There isn't too much I remember from that day, but I do remember speaking up. I do remember sounds which somehow formed words coming out of my mouth and explaining through trembling voice what happened to me that day on the beach that changed the trajectory of my life forever.

Sometimes speaking up isn't easy. Sometimes it requires digging deep, acknowledging that inner tremble and pushing through it anyways. It requires knowing even without understanding how or why, that your voice, your truth is worth hearing.

This means speaking up at work. It means speaking up for yourself in your relationships, with a friend and within yourself. It means that even if it is scary as shit, even if all roads seem to point to run the other way, that you dig your heels into the ground beneath you and say what needs to be said. Yes, some might not even hear you. And yes, you might lose some people along the way. But if in your soul you know this is the right thing, then summon up that voice of yours to rise to the top and speak up as if your life is dependent on it. It just might very well be.

I spent way too many years smiling and keeping things inside or passive aggressively making 'jokes' to keep from ruffling any feathers. Ruffle them! Sometimes they need a new style. Now of course, I'm not speaking about being reckless with others. I'm not talking about bullying or walking over or even strong holding anyone. (I think you know this, but I have to state this for clarity's sake.) I'm saying that if your soul is speaking to you to speak up, you honor that voice within by bringing it out.

We all know there are moments when we choose to not speak up because we are afraid what someone else might think. We are afraid we will upset someone. Will we end up alone? Will we end up in a place that feels scary? Maybe! But you also will end up in a place *you* feel good in, one with integrity, self-worth and self-esteem. You will be living from a space that you can be proud of. And before you know it, the discomfort passes, and you will begin attracting more people and more situations in your life that you really want. You will begin to wake up to the fact that you deserve more, and that no matter how much your voice might be trembling, there is serenity in your soul.

Now that's worth shouting from the rooftop!

⛽ FUEL UP

On the road to self-love, there will be moments that you are being called to show up and speak up. Through sweaty palms and racing heart, you show up and speak up like the mother f'n badass that you are. Yeah, I said it! Now what?

Psst—go easy on yourself.

Rest Stop 13

STOP TRYING
TO BE PERFECT

This need to not make mistakes and be perfect has ruled me my entire life. It has kept me safe on the inside while on the outside it seemed like a pattern of daring career choices. It has kept me safe in terms of always choosing relationships that couldn't work out one way or another. It has kept me safe during the years I spent hiding behind my obese body. This need to not make mistakes for fear of being hurt took over my entire life. And the one thing that I kept being shown was that playing it safe kept me bored. It kept me feeling discontent, disconnected, anxious and feeling un-alive.

When I found myself in the hands of my abuser, I didn't know what choices to make in that moment. The only thing I did know was that I wanted to stay safe. So, safety for me showed up as not screaming. It showed up as not being forceful or truthful in my responses. And safety for me showed up as not stopping him for fear of what he would do to me. So, I learned to make safe choices in my life believing that would ultimately get me through safely.

But that's not where it ended. This obsession with not making mistakes was born out of feeling that I had been blamed for what happened to me. To be clear, the people in my life did not outwardly blame me. However, they did pose questions to me, make comments to me and the deafening silence at times surrounding the event made me feel this way. I then came to believe that if I went through life not being 'naïve' and if I went through life making safer choices and not making mistakes, I wouldn't be hurt again. And that is where the perfectionist was born. I tried so hard to do everything right.

Along with trying to get the world to like me, perfectionism ranks right up there as one of my hardest lessons. As mentioned at the start, this book has been held off for years now simply because I had to make it perfect. And since that's impossible, I didn't fully commit to writing this. I only showed up every few months for it. I spoke about it. I would refer to it. But when it came to sitting my ass down and really committing to it, there was no way I was going to finish it because there was no way I would *ever* put something out there that wasn't just right (perfect).

Buckle up! This is harsh to hear, and I apologize in advance, but you are not perfect, either. Gasp! I know. I know. It's still hard for me to accept sometimes. So much so that I still can feel anxiety around things I have to do because of the expectations I'm putting on myself. But here's the thing I'm proud to say now—I am learning how to jump off before I slide down that slippery slope that takes me away into the crazy land of trying so damn hard to be perfect.

When I sense that I'm approaching that slope, I give myself pep talks. Yup, I sure do. I remind myself that all I have to do is just try. I remind myself that all I have to do is *show up* for this task, for this moment, for this anything. And no matter the outcome, I won't die. These words on this paper (perfect or not), do not determine my worth.

Perfection…
IT DOES NOT EXIST IN ANYONE.
Yes–those caps are on purpose. I am yelling. Not at you–at the entire world. Just STOP.

If you set these ridiculous expectations of perfection, you will always be disappointed in yourself. It's too damn exhausting to feel that way all the time and to have to crawl yourself out of that self-pity hole time and time again. At some point you can catch on and realize that whatever bar you keep setting for yourself, it's never high enough. Stop the crazy chase! (And if it's not perfectionism for you, insert whatever else you keep chasing.)

While I would love for you to be so crazy inspired by every 'perfect' word I write and that you take action to completely transform your life, the truth is that not only is that impossible, it means that anything else I do in life has to exceed that perfection I've already attained. And it would absolutely give me a coronary to have to even begin to think about taking that on. So, for now, I'll just show up doing my best and in the times that it's not so great, I'll love myself anyway.

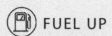 FUEL UP

On the road to self-love, do the best you can. Show up. Be kind. Love hard. Be honest. Have fun. And when you screw up, apologize. There is no perfect person out there and once you give up on trying to be that, you'll come to see that who you are is good enough. Just keep being more of you. More of your perfectly, imperfect self.

Psst–go easy on yourself.

Rest Stop 14

SECRET TO LIFE

"Do you want to know the secret to life?"

"Huh?" I thought.

I was completely perplexed by this question and I must've had this confused look on my face because he repeated it again, but this time much slower. "Do...you...want...to...know...the...secret...to...life?" Now, of course, a question like that begs for a long pause. It's such a loaded question for a girl in her early teens and it was the first time my uncle ever started a real conversation with me.

We used to go to my aunt and uncle's house a few times a month. My family was very small, but we certainly made up for it by being big in personality. The women overpowered the men both in talking and in size. Let's just say they didn't have any trouble expressing what they thought and how they felt, even if it wasn't what you wanted to hear.

... except for my uncle. He has always been a very quiet and understated man. Growing up, I really didn't ever know what to say to him. He was usually planted on the couch watching television or in his 'computer room' simply in awe of what it could do. I was in awe that he named the entire room after this machine that sat on a desk. He would politely greet us all when we come over and then quickly go back to whatever he was doing.

From the beginning, I picked up on energy. I didn't realize it until many years later, but what I noticed is that I especially gravitated towards warm and inviting energy and when I didn't feel that, there was a discomfort of sorts and I wouldn't know how to interact and engage. As I got older, that all changed and it sort of became a game for me to 'turn' someone over to the 'light' side.

We were on one of our weekend visits and out of nowhere, my uncle said, "Come with me, Shari. I want to share something important with you." I felt like I was a cartoon character doing a double-take as I wondered if he was actually referring to *me*. Since I was the only Shari in the room, I knew it had to be me. I wasn't sure what to do or think but I do remember being nervous to take that walk into the other room. My heart was thumping rapidly, and my mind was going a million miles a minute wondering what was he going to say. What was so important and more importantly, how was I going to respond? I honestly had never had a deep conversation with him and so I had no idea what to expect.

I followed him into the den, and he turned right around to me, looked me dead in the eyes and asked the question. "Do you want to know the secret to life?" I remember thinking, "No warmup question? No intro? No 'I know we never, ever talk but...'"

Nope. None of that! The *secret* to life!

Did I want to know it? Of course, I did! But I was still in shock that we were even conversing and even more in shock that this was the first time he really spoke to me. When he finally had something to say to me, he laid something this heavy on me. And then I began wondering *why* was he sharing this with me? Why was I being given this very important information and what was I supposed to do with it? I casually said, "Sure," as if what he was about to share with me was as normal as sharing the weather forecast.

He paused for what seemed like an eternity and began moving his mouth with each word coming out very deliberately, "That which you think most about you will become." His face lit up like I had never seen before. He knew that he had just shared something huge! He sat there waiting for my equally impressed look back. I don't know if I looked impressed or just confused by that secret or still shocked that we were actually talking. I must've had some blank stare on my face because he then repeated it back, "That which you think most about you will become." Then he quickly turned around and walked out and back to the living room and went back to watching TV while I was left with this life secret to comprehend.

Side note: This was shared with me in the late 1980's, so the movie or book, *The Secret,* wasn't out yet. Here he was sharing with me THE secret! Until this moment, I didn't even put that together that he was sharing with me the secret to life before *The Secret* ever came out.

To be honest, I am not sure if I had a clue what that meant (besides what seemed like the obvious) and so I remember spending the rest of that day with my family thinking and concentrating *really* hard on becoming an actress. If this was really the secret to life, I was thinking my way into fame! I also spent the rest of that day wondering why he chose to share this seemingly very important secret with me.

Many decades later, I do understand and am so grateful for the gift that was given to me that day. I understand the magnitude of what he was sharing. What you give your attention to—good or bad—you will become. You will live it, experience it and will attract it.

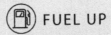 **FUEL UP**

On the road to self-love, be mindful of your mind. Indulge yourself with kind thoughts and beautiful ideas. Gentle words and loving support. Allow peace in and spread goodness out. Be compassionate with yourself as you move through life's challenges and remember that what you allow into your sacred space within, grows there. Make sure you love what you're planting.

Psst—go easy on yourself.

Rest Stop 15

PSST! LOOSEN YOUR GRIP

I used to hold onto things (men) for dear life. And by hold on to them, I mean keep pushing things way past their expiration date. While everything inside me told me that they weren't the 'one' for me, I gripped tighter. If you can imagine having someone wrapped around your ankle as you are trying to walk out the door, that was me. I held on longer than I should have, grasping them and trying to force them to stay.

Of course, I wasn't that obvious about it. I mean, I didn't want to seem desperate. The truth was, I just kept adapting and sacrificing myself and my needs so I could hold them in place. The idea of someone leaving me out here in the world alone was terrifying to me. I wasn't aware of that at the time, but after a whole lot of soul searching, it's the only thing that truly explains this fear of someone leaving me.

Truth be told, I gripped a whole lot of things besides just relationships. I stayed in jobs longer than I should have. I held on to extra weight longer than I should have. Basically, I tried to hold everything in place because any outward disruption would cause a whole helluva lot of inward destruction. And I know I'm not alone in this. I see you, too, white knuckler.

I totally get it and understand you. It makes sense to try to hold onto things as they are because the idea of change is so freaking scary. You've gotten comfortable where you are. You know how people show up and respond to you. You know what to expect from yourself and from life. It makes perfect sense, except the fact that you're freaking miserable! Okay, maybe not to that extreme, but there just might be a constant nagging feeling within you that something is just off. And you keep ignoring it because then all your comforts will go away, and you'll have to face that discomfort within. Plus, it's maybe not 'that' bad. So, it seems easier to just keep things as they are because you're just 'fine' with how things are.

But here's the rub in all of this. While you are so busy holding on for dear life to what you currently have, your dreams trying to come into fruition are being pushed away. The prayers you've sent out are trying to be answered but you're holding onto what you currently have out of fear of what 'might' come. Nothing can make its way in because you've closed yourself off.

This all came to a head for me when I scurried off to Italy to 'find' myself. I remember waking up one morning and this deep desire to hold people and ideals in place somehow seemed not as important. Something shifted. It was so exhausting trying to hold onto things that obviously weren't meant to be. It was as if I finally released open the prison gate and allowed everyone and everything out of it. The only thing that can explain this sudden shift within was watching myself be by myself throughout that summer. I was finding my way, discovering my likes and dislikes and ultimately seeing that I could and always would be okay by myself. Let me explain a little bit better.

This is a passage out of my journal from that summer…

Lesson in letting go is getting easier every single day. Trying to hold onto people and things that just aren't meant for me (or just don't make me feel good), I've been learning to release. Not only release but let go without any negative feelings towards me. Thoughts like, "What's wrong with me?", "Why wasn't I chosen?", "Am I not good enough?", are no longer running on repeat in my mind. I'm learning with letting go that some things just aren't meant for me. And that's okay because that just means I'm a step closer to what is meant for me.

I think I've always known this 'logically', but now I'm experiencing it and watching myself make beautiful and healthy decisions for myself. I know so much of that has to do with seeing my ways of being in the world, how much I have to offer the world, and also how much any job, any man, any 'anything' would be blessed to have me in their life. Feeling that feeling for myself and not just saying it because it's the "positive" and "right" thing to think or say is so beautiful and freeing for me—just a wonderful, wonderful feeling to have for myself.

(8/13/2013 journal entry)

What I came to discover that summer was that when I was willing to trust myself and God, the things that were meant for me would find their way to me if I remained open. It became a lot easier to let the things fall away that were ultimately not good for me.

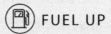 **FUEL UP**

On the road to self-love, be willing to put your 'security' blanket away. Be willing to part with your big ol' ratty and torn 'security' blanket that actually isn't even doing its job properly. Trust that your dreams and prayers have been answered and are right here if you're willing to loosen your grip and allow them in. What's waiting inside those clenched fists of yours is a life that is anything but miserable!

Psst—go easy on yourself.

DO IT YOUR OWN SELF!

"You are everything I've ever needed. There is no one else on this earth I'd rather wake up to other than you. I can't imagine my life without you."

Pretty romantic, huh? This is all I ever wanted to hear. These beautiful words filled with drippings of praise and affection that would make me feel loved, worthy and special. Such words would ease and settle the unease and chaos within me. So, when I received this acknowledgement, I couldn't understand for the life of me why I still wasn't happy, why it *still* wasn't enough. Why did I still hear that voice within that echoed, "It's not enough." Can you relate to getting everything you ever said you wanted and it still not being what you need?

What I came to find out after years of getting what I said I wanted from some external source and still not being satisfied was that what I was longing for and desperately needing could never be filled by him or anyone or anything. He could say all the romantic and perfect things, and while on the surface it could fill what I thought I needed temporarily, after some time it just wouldn't be enough. I'd become numb to it, maybe even disinterested. This wasn't because I didn't love him, but because what I had been longing for is a feeling that only I could satiate. The love I wanted someone to express to me was more about making me feel safe and secure within the world. This is simply not anything that anyone else could ever do for me. I had to find that myself and come to a place of inner peace within.

We so often go into relationships, chase money and careers searching for these things to fill what seems like internal bottomless wounds. We look to others and to things to be our saviors. Please stop. Beautiful soul, it's not fair to them and it's a waste of time for you.

 FUEL UP

On the road to self-love, nobody will ever be able to fill those holes within or satiate your deepest desires. Nobody else will ever be able to give you what only you can give yourself. Start within and create an inner world that begins and ends with **your love**.

Psst–go easy on yourself.

Rest Stop 17

SHUT UP & LISTEN

This chapter is dedicated to all you smarty-pants—the wellness gurus, the self-help book readers, workshop attendees and personal development junkies. Yes, you.

I know you know how to analyze yourself. I know you know what you *should* be thinking or how you *should* be reacting (oops, 'responding') in any given situation. I get it. I am the queen of knowing all the 'right' things to do and say when certain situations arise. However, when it came to really showing up for myself on a deeper level, I glossed my way right through that baby!

I applied every little healing trick I knew. At the very first sign of some internal discomfort, I got to work! I pulled out all the stops! I did mirror work, affirmations, journaling, forgiveness exercises and anything else I could find to do. Now, unless you *really* know what is at the core of your pain, using all these healing tools is sort of like putting a Band-Aid over a deep cut. Don't get me wrong. These are great tools—except I missed the very first and most important step in true and lasting healing. It turned out to be the simplest and powerful step.

Listening.

... quieting our mind, asking the right questions and then having the willingness to sit and listen to the answer. It's not always about trying to figure out a solution. Perhaps all you and I are being called to do is just shut up and listen. There are such deep messages in stillness. There's so much healing in that quiet space. But when you're trying to apply everything you know and everything you've learned to every situation, you lose out on the gift we've been given which is simply to surrender and listen.

And man, that's a hard one for us overachievers. I wanted to figure out why everything, every challenge and every back step was showing up for me. For years, I just wanted to understand and analyze it all. Finally, I came to realize that all the work I was doing continually pointed me back to myself. It was calling to the stillness and quiet within me. Everything that was showing up and that I was willing to listen to was asking me to spend more time within myself and sit with my pain. To hear it. To comfort it. To forgive it and to love it. But I would've never known this because I was too busy trying to fix it.

Now, I know it's not nice to say the words "shut up", but in this particular situation with the most love and respect I can muster for you, shut up.

And of course, *listen*.

 FUEL UP:

On the road to self-love, shhhhhh.

Psst—go easy on yourself.

Rest Stop 18

THE LESSONS KEEP ON COMING

For the last few weeks, I've been feeling more anxious than I have in some time. It's the type of anxiety you can't seem to release. The one that sticks to you like *it* has separation anxiety. (Great, my anxiety has anxiety and so does its host. This doesn't look good.) I wake with it. I go to bed with it. And the worst thing is that I can't seem to explain it. There are no conscious thoughts as to what I could be grappling with or what seems to be holding me hostage. Right before this happened, I was having all these revelations! I understood why I had been feeling so sick, why I was making certain choices and I was confident that now that I knew all this everything would finally fall into place.

I understood it all!

And just when you feel like you have it all finally figured out and you're on the path to feeling better, wouldn't you know it, a dump truck comes and unloads some new crap on you and everything you were just certain of, comes crashing down and looks like a complete stranger flattened out in front of you. Sound familiar?

It happens to most of us but let me assure you of this. This doesn't happen because you're unlucky or undeserving or a failure. It happens because there's another layer for you to uncover. Another layer to heal. Perhaps you just scratched the surface and you're not quite there yet. But the good news is that you're on your way!

These new challenges arrive to show us that we have more excavating to do. We just aren't at master level yet. It's sort of like that pop quiz in school that would test what you just finished reading or studying in order to really know if you've learned it. Part of this journey we take in life is about always evolving, always peeling another layer away, always growing and becoming more connected with you. And that sometimes comes along with what seems like a dump truck of crap; which really is a treasure that just needs to be dusted off and polished.

So, while this anxiety might have come back to hang with me for a bit, I'm confident that by simply giving it *more* love, *more* patience and *more* compassion, what is triggering it will be coaxed to rise to the surface. Then I can love on it and nurture what is clearly begging for my attention.

 FUEL UP

On the road to self-love, be open to learning! Know that with every new experience comes another lesson. And when that lesson isn't fully learned, another experience will come to make sure that you really get it this time. It's like a parent offering tough love. Embrace the love. And if you don't want to be nagged by it again, take the time to learn the lesson.

Now, back to my own continued lesson. Stillness. See ya at the next stop!

Psst—go easy on yourself.

Rest Stop 19

STOP WAITING FOR OTHERS TO MAKE YOU FEEL GOOD

I remember scrolling through what seemed like an endless feed of people telling me how wonderful I was, how inspiring I was, how beautiful, amazing, how much of a light, a savior even. I read every single word and I didn't feel anything–not one emotion. I didn't even feel indifference. I only felt numbness. I kept scrolling and words just kept coming at me and *nothing*. My entire life I have searched for self-worth in what others thought about me and said about me and here these thoughts and words were literally right in my face and *nothing*!

The truth is that there wasn't a compliment alive that would've changed this feeling or lack of feeling inside me. There wasn't a person in the world that could try to convince me. It finally hit me as I was staring at these words from others, "Shari, YOU don't feel this way about yourself."

This hit me like a ton of bricks. I could barely breathe as I took in what it meant. I mean, here I had been my entire life seeking approval and love and here it was right in my face, and it meant absolutely nothing.

I didn't know what to do or think. I didn't know where to begin or what was wrong with me. Why don't I feel anything? Am I numb to life? Has my heart gone cold? I remember putting my phone away and just staring for hours at my bedroom ceiling. And then, in the midst of my panic over whether I had turned into a robot, I noticed that a part of me actually felt relieved. I mean, if I didn't care about what others thought, then I could somehow be let off the hook of trying to do everything for everyone and finally just *live*! Shit! I think some big shift just happened!

Of course, it wasn't all this crystal clear to me in that exact moment. What was clear, however, was that I had just been given a gift. Somehow, in some small way, the ground beneath me shifted a bit. Some movement happened within and it was so subtle–like a leaf gently being lifted off the ground by a small breeze. But man, was it ever so powerful.

Up to that point, I was relying on someone else to tell me how wonderful I was. For someone else to tell me how much I was needed and valued. Every relationship I went into wasn't about them; rather it was about how they would make *me* feel. And it's hard to admit that. It's hard to be that honest with yourself. But within that raw honesty and discovery lay the ability to transform that and then find the love I was actually seeking within.

⛽ FUEL UP

On the road to self-love, if you're finding yourself in relationships wishing that they would say something else, do something else, be someone else–perhaps what you're seeking is only something that you can give yourself. No person, no thing, no goal achieved will ever make you feel a certain way about yourself until you do.

"Stop waiting for others to tell you how great you are. Believe it for yourself and about yourself." -Iyanla Vanzant

Psst–go easy on yourself.

Rest Stop 20

WHAT YOU WANT ISN'T ALWAYS WHAT YOU NEED

The entire year leading up to my thirtieth birthday, I was in full on feeling-sorry-for-myself-what-is-wrong-with-me-pathetic-girl crisis. That might sound harsh, but if you had seen the entirety of my journal, I assure you that I'm being nice with how I just described myself.

Don't believe me? Check this out.

Feeling pathetically weak again. More importantly just dumb. Does it take a stronger person to stay in the same situation and take on the pain, or is it stronger to step away from the situation and deal with that pain? I think I already know the answer to that. However, my mind changes every day! One day I feel strong and am going to make all these changes and other times I feel lazy and complacent. Aaah! I am almost 30! I know it's

*just a number but it's time I grew up! I don't need
so much attention! Damn, Shari. Get it together
already.*

(4/27/2003 journal entry)

Poor girl. I was so confused, so seeking approval and love, and just feeling desperate for someone to see me and love me. I was even writing love letters to myself because I was needing that so badly. Plus, it felt really good imagining that someone actually felt that way about me.

But in between those self-scribed love letters lay these overwhelming thoughts and questions.

"What is wrong with me?"
"Why did he choose her and not me?"
"How come she got the part and I didn't?"

The one thing I have discovered over the many, many, (did I mention many?) years of asking these questions ad nauseam is that the majority of times things didn't go my way, it wasn't because there was anything wrong with me; rather it was because everything was right with me. The job, the relationship, the turned down loan for a car, all of it, every single 'no' and every single closed door happened because those things weren't meant for me. There was something else that was. I was supposed to learn something else, discover something great, be something better.

There hasn't been a moment that I've looked back at my life in hindsight and thought, man, I wish something else would've happened instead. You know why? Because *everything* has turned out better. Yeah, maybe it takes longer than we want. Maybe the journey is filled with more detours than straightaways. But ending up in a relationship that you ultimately aren't happy in and ending up in a job that stifles you and ending up in a friendship that uses you isn't worth settling in simply because it hurts too much in the moment to let it go. So, those detours while you figure your stuff out are absolutely necessary.

The thing is, beautiful soul, not everything is meant for you. One day you will awaken to the fact that you've been using all your precious energy trying to squeeze a circle into a triangle. You will realize that you spend all your time convincing yourself why you should stay in the relationship, how they might wake up and realize your value, how the job might get better, the friendship will improve, the 'this' will do that...

Guess what? Sometimes it just doesn't and sometimes it just isn't.

You are too special to have to try to make someone like you.

(5/11/2003 journal entry)

 **FUEL UP**

On the road to self-love, being completely honest with yourself is going to break you open. And then it's going to allow you to be where you're supposed to be and with whom is meant for you. It is in the trusting, the loosening of your grip, and surrendering what you think you want, when you finally settle down and feel like you're sitting in the perfect space and in your perfect skin.

Things finally make sense and you feel like you can breathe again.

There is nothing wrong with you, beautiful one.

There is nothing you need to change except the amount you love yourself.

Love yourself until full.

Love yourself until you can't love anymore.

Psst—go easy on yourself.

Rest Stop 21

SURRENDER

It was 2013 and I remember laying on my bed in my cute apartment in West Hollywood overlooking the Hollywood Hills and thinking that I finally had it all together. I met the man who loved me, saw me and understood me. We were planning to move in together, which was a huge step for me as I had never lived full-time with a guy before. I was skinnier than I had ever been. I was feeling more confident, and I was excited to see where my acting career would take me now that I was feeling more like *me*. Things were looking up!

So, when he broke up with me, my seemingly upside up world was suddenly turned downside up and it felt like somebody had danced the cha-cha-cha all over my heart. Yeah, you could say I was crushed. I didn't get it. I couldn't understand why God would have me open my heart to him, the heart that was deeply afraid to trust, to then have me feel discarded, ditched and worth walking away from. I was so deeply wounded by this. Every part of me thought that this had to be a cruel joke, so I began questioning my faith.

Now up to this point, I was well-seasoned at saying that I fully trusted God. I remember spouting these words out and speaking about faith, being taken care of and always being loved and supported. And yet, when shit would hit the fan, I'd freak the hell out! I lost sleep. I dealt with anxiety. I questioned everything. Myself especially, but even God.

In order to keep things neatly packaged so that these moments wouldn't take me by surprise, I spent most of my adult life trying to control the outcome of situations. And what exactly did this look like? It looked like being aggravated and upset when people didn't act how I expected them to act or say what I wanted them to say. So, I laid some guilt on them. I told them how they *should* show up in my life and what they *should* be saying if they truly loved me.

It also showed up as self-disappointment in not achieving what I thought I needed to be doing. It showed up as hurt when I felt like I was being judged, when I chose men who I knew would disappoint me because I already knew that I'd be disappointed. When you know what to expect, you don't have other expectations. So, I dated the men who were unavailable emotionally and physically. I tried to create and control everything in my life so that I wouldn't feel out of control or unsafe ever again. Now of course, as you can imagine, there's no way to humanly do that because there are so many variables and factors at play.

Surrender is truly the only thing I've ever done, chosen and not manipulated that has truly made me feel safe.

Surrender ultimately means to wave the white flag. It means to lay down arms, open your heart, close your eyes and lay back and float down the river of life knowing that you will arrive wherever you need to be as safely as you need to be.

Surrender is the true and ultimate expression of self-love. It's trusting who you are, what you've learned and what will be there for you when you let your guard down. Surrender is sending a message to yourself that's saying, "I love you. I trust in you and I trust in something even greater than you that will continue to take care and provide for you."

I know it's scary. I know throwing your hands up in the air and announcing that you are going to release all expectations and outcomes and are choosing to trust, even though you've been hurt and betrayed and disappointed in your life. I know how freaking scary that is. But the alternative is living a life sheltered and filled with fear all in the pursuit of trying to hold it together, so you're not left vulnerable and open.

Surrender can seem messy. Usually when you've chosen the route of surrender, it's because when you look around, your life looks like a pool of disorder and chaos. And so, you throw in the towel, drop to your knees and you finally surrender. It's not surprising that you initially feel unsafe and insecure in that surrender because you're already deep in the throws of what feels like a shit storm. What if in the chaos and messy simply lies the rearranging of your life? Perhaps you've gotten off track and off your path, and so God is simply rearranging things to put you back on the path towards your dreams.

What if surrender has nothing to do with giving up something, but rather receiving everything?

I wish with all my heart that I could give you a step-by-step process on how to make all this easier. The only way I know how to do that is simply by trusting, which as you know, from my other chapter on safety, is and has not been the easiest thing for me. And this of course, makes it ironic that these are the two lessons I've had to deal with simultaneously in my life.

As mentioned above, I'm still learning this. I've worked hard at surrendering, which sounds funny because where is the surrender in 'working hard'? In all fairness, I've gotten better at this. I'm learning to not only recognize the way I'm feeling but to also invite that feeling to have a voice (even if it doesn't always feel good). The more I allow myself to be witness to these states and emotions, the more I can see that they aren't so bad. Then the need to control outcomes or situations begins to lessen.

When you spend your life trying to control who others are, how they show up in your life and the circumstances that surround you, you miss out on the magic and mystery and unbelievable beauty that life is.

Learning to release your hold on things and people only comes from trusting that when you do, what shows up for you are the things and people that are meant to be in your life. It comes from trusting that the situations you encounter are there to help you grow and expand. It comes from trusting the life you ultimately are meant to live is showing up for you. Giving up control is truly about surrendering to the idea that you don't know everything and no matter how hard you try, force or manipulate things, the outcome ultimately is going to be what is meant to be. Either you can fight and force your way through it, or you can throw up your arms and allow yourself to be carried.

I know. I hear you. That's why I'm still working on this part. But man, I certainly breathe and feel better when I do.

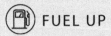 FUEL UP

On the road to self-love, trust and not fear is what will have you walking more surefooted in this world. By trusting enough to finally surrender, your journey to self-love will be one that feels like an incredible gift that somehow you were lucky enough to be given.

Psst–go easy on yourself.

Rest Stop 22

BUCK UP BABY, THE TRUTH HURTS

(BUT YOU GET USED TO IT)

"The truth hurts." I used to hate when somebody would say that to me like they knew me, or they knew what I was thinking. I mean I hated it to the point where it would turn into arguments. The reality was, I hated it because there was truth to it. It triggered me. It touched some pain point within me and that made me bark back like a rabid dog. (Okay, maybe more of an annoying Yorkie, but you get the point.)

When someone said something to me that resonated and that I wasn't ready to deal with yet, I got defensive. I made it about them—*their* insecurities, *their* issues, *their* doubts. Then I stomped away like a five-year-old having a temper tantrum. Then without fail, like a sorrowful and regretful puppy, I returned letting them know that I thought about it and not only was I sorry, that maybe somewhere deep inside, there was a slight taste of truth.

Now for me, the reason why I didn't want to face this truth is not because I didn't want to be wrong in their eyes. It was because I didn't want to be wrong in *my* eyes. I didn't want to have to face yet another thing I had to deal with. So, I simply chose not to by denying it. Hmmph! I showed them.

Here's the thing about truths–they can hurt, but you get used to it. You get used to the feeling that you aren't always right. You get used to the feeling that you don't have to always be right and even more so, you kind of like the feeling of learning new things about yourself. Now let's not jump ahead of ourselves. It's not like I loved being told that certain things I said had hurt others or certain actions I took had bothered someone; but I *did* love being able to fix it and to be able to see myself and others more clearly.

And guess what? The more truths I allowed myself to hear, the more I stopped making decisions that were against *my* deep core truths. I took more actions that were aligned with my heart and that began a ripple of having to hear less and less about these 'truths.' You see how that works?

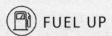 FUEL UP

On the road to self-love, the more you're willing to explore your inner world and become self-aware, the more you live a life that feels good. You become more secure in who you are and what you want. Then the life you lead reflects and aligns with your values and your ultimate goals.

So yes, spit those truths at me. But please, be gentle, too.

Psst–go easy on yourself.

Rest Stop 23

VULNERABILITY IS BEAUTIFUL

I was waiting tables at a fancy steakhouse in Hollywood, CA while pursuing an acting career (not a stereotype at all) and, as in any restaurant if you've ever worked in one, you become close with your coworkers. Everyone is working towards something else and everyone shows up each day not really wanting to be there. We all make the best of it, but we also are all driven and passionate people who are following their hearts calling. So, you become close in this common pursuit.

I remember one particular day standing at the bar station waiting for a couple of drinks and chatting away about something probably inappropriate to most, and my manager leaned in towards me. All I saw was his hand moving towards my face and more specifically my hair and I jumped back as if some big explosion had happened. He looked at me with a confused look on his face (probably also a bit scared of me) and said, "There was a piece of lint in your hair." To most, they would've been thankful. Not me.

I wear a wig.

It was/is something that I'm always aware of. I'm always wondering if the fake hairline is showing, or if it's on crooked. Or maybe a wind gust will come and mess it up or blow it off. I think about will someone hug me and pull it off as they embrace me. Or will someone go to pull a piece of lint off my hair and end up with all of my hair in their hand…

So yeah, needless to say, I was paranoid about it. The only thing that seemed to make sense and was instinctual for me was to jump and slightly freak out. I hadn't told anyone there that I wore a wig, not even this group of people that I felt super close to. It wasn't that I didn't trust them; it was simply that I wasn't ready to face that truth myself. I wasn't ready to deal with what others might think of me. Would they suddenly not see me in the same way they did before? Would I be judged? Would I be less liked? It seemed so utterly important at the time to hide this and, looking back now, all I can do is laugh at how unimportant it all really was and how much time I spent brooding over things that ultimately didn't matter in the long run.

Here's the thing. We all are hiding something, ashamed of something, or wishing we could share something. And here's the bigger thing. When we do come clean, everyone around us suddenly feels better. Everyone around us feels less alone and realizes that they, too, are able to open up, accept and embrace all of themselves. Vulnerability is everything. It's beautiful! It saves lives. It brings people closer together.

 FUEL UP

On the road to self-love, your willingness to stand in your truth, own your imperfections and stand butt-ass naked in your authenticity is everything. It's what makes you you and allows others to truly embrace not only you, but themselves even more. Do not ever be afraid to share what's in your heart–even the hard things–especially the hard things. Those who love you will love you even more and those who are uncomfortable with it are most likely uncomfortable in their own skin. One day they will open up and it will be because you were brave enough to be **you**.

P.S. I ended up telling my coworkers about my hair. Not just them, but most of the world. I blogged about it. Then I made a very public video about it and now I pretty much tell anyone who compliments me on my hair. "Oh, thank you! It's a wig!"

Psst–go easy on yourself.

Rest Stop 24

LIFE WILL KNOCK YOU ON YOUR ASS (LITERALLY!)

I remember it was early 2003 and I was devastated over why my 'friend' didn't like me back and why I wasn't enough for him. We (he) had decided to take a break and stop talking. I guessed it was because I might have been 'too' much. Whatever! He used to talk to me all day long and had all the time in the world for me. Then he went and got himself a girlfriend and he ignored me. I hated being ignored! And if you ignored me, then yes, I would send you some (57) texts wondering why you weren't answering me! Take a hint, Shari! But I couldn't. Deep down I felt dispensable and I hated feeling like I meant nothing.

So, my journal began filling up with declarations of how I was going to move on!…"That's it! I am better than this!" And then progressed into how I had moved on!…"I don't need him anymore! Screw him!" And then they changed to how I was back to not moving on…"Why doesn't he like me?" Sigh. That was the pattern in my life–the continual knowing what I should do, then not doing it and then being disappointed and then trying again until something literally would stop me. And I mean literally.

Some time had gone by since my 'friend' and I had stopped speaking when I found out that we were both invited to a mutual friend's barbecue. I was super nervous about seeing him and wondered if I should even go at all. I spent the days leading up to this event convincing myself that this would be good. We would finally talk, and all would be okay. I didn't even care that his girlfriend would probably be there. I just wanted to be friends again! Oh, who the hell was I kidding? Inside I was secretly hoping that he would see me and realize how much he missed me, would dump his ugly girlfriend and all would be right in the world. Yeah, the normal psycho stuff. I spent half the day praying that when I saw him, I would say and do the right thing. I told God that I gave it over to Him and whatever was supposed to happen would. (Hopefully God was on my side and would do what I mentioned above.)

The following is an entry taken out of my journal from that evening right before the barbecue:

Well, I guess I didn't need to make any decisions about going to the BBQ. I slipped in the shower and re-injured my knee. Now I can barely walk.

(5/14/03 journal entry)

So, here's the thing. For many years, I was making the same bad choices again and again. I was given warning after warning until I would get knocked on my ass. It's the only time I ever stopped those patterns.

Note to you: *Do not do this*!

Once you get the first message, *listen*. Follow that guidance. It starts as a little whisper, a soft nudge or a quiet voice. You know, "Hey, I have a girlfriend now." If you choose to ignore it, that whisper gets a bit louder. "Hey, you're too crazy. Let's not talk." And if you choose to ignore that, it usually shows up in the form of some 2x4 hitting you upside the head or in my case, falling in the shower and tearing your ligament and not being able to walk.

That wasn't the first or last time I was forced into or out of a situation where I didn't belong. I continued to push the limits, ignore the signs and reap all the consequences (broken hearts, health issues, etc.). Then one day, just like Forrest Gump, I stopped. I was tired. I was tired of getting beaten up and tired of finding myself in the same place again and again. I began to pay closer attention to my inner whispers. I began to notice when they showed up and I actually chose to listen. Was I perfect? Nah. I had some more bumps and bruises that showed up, but I didn't learn overnight how to be this way, so it wasn't an overnight process to unlearn it either. I'm happy to report that I no longer require any 2x4's to force me back to center.

 FUEL UP

On the road to self-love, you are always being guided and given direction. You are always looked out for and looked after. Return the kind gesture by paying attention and then taking action.

Psst—go easy on yourself.

Rest Stop 25

CHOOSE TRUST

It took me a very long time to move on from Mike*–five thousand, four hundred and ninety-three days to be exact. That's how long I remained single. Please don't feel sorry for me. I had plenty of flings throughout that time, but in the opening my heart and trusting again department, that took time. The truth was that I had no idea how I was going to get through this. I could barely breathe moment to moment, so the idea that I would ever come out the other side seemed light years away.

For the first time in many years (since pre-abuse), I finally felt safe and secure in this relationship. I didn't for the life of me ever expect this to happen. Yet here I was trying to figure out how I was going to move on after his infidelity. His cheating! I was dumbfounded and utterly confused. It never dawned on me that I wasn't the one for him. I mean, all my friends even told me that *he* was the lucky one. *He* was the one that got the grand prize! (Now that's just dumb saying that but we were in our teens and so I just believed it.)

During the months and years that followed, I obsessed over the idea of him coming back to me. I imagined how he was going to wake up one day and realize that he couldn't live without me and that he was suffering and made the biggest mistake. I convinced myself that he would return because 'absence makes the heart grow fonder' and how if you set someone free, yada yada yada. I held on to this idea for so long while holding up my life for so long.

One day I stopped wishing and stopped crying. I had made it out the other side. Something inside hurt just a little bit less. I continued healing and one day I remember thinking, "Thank God I didn't marry him." Yeah, that was a big one for me. I learned from this experience and countless others that if you choose to trust in your life and what is happening at that moment, even if you don't fully understand it, then you ultimately make your journey a whole lot easier. You stop questioning. You stop feeling sorry for yourself. You stop suffering.

Then one day it hit me like a bolt of lightning. I realized that I should stop waiting for hindsight to trust what was happening. When I came out the other side of something that didn't work out, I learned that it ultimately wasn't a good situation. And I bet that I'm not alone. I bet there are quite a few moments in your life that didn't work out and now you can see the blessing in them not working out. I have since decided that when unexpected things happen, I trust them–even if it hurts. This not only feels better (although stuff still hurts), but it allows you to move through things with more grace and more ease.

Change is inevitable. You can try to control it. You can try to manipulate it. You can try to stronghold it and keep what is in place, but the blessing in change is that it brings forth a new you. It uncovers parts of you that may have been lying dormant. It challenges you and can bring out the best in you.

Now, you might not always be comfortable with change. More than likely, you probably will be terrified of it because you simply don't recognize what has shown up. Life often presents not what you want, but what you *need*. Up to this point, you were probably praying for something else. Then this package arrives not looking anything like what you were expecting and so you ignore it. For me, I ignored it for a couple of years.

My current fiancé (maybe husband by the time you read this), John, showed up as the most unrecognizable package (no insult intended, hon). Right before he came along, I was surrounded with people (men, specifically) who didn't always respect me. I'm fairly certain I didn't respect myself and so I attracted those who didn't as well. However, there was this big part of me that desired more for myself than I was currently giving myself and a smaller part of me that knew that I deserved better. Although it was a tiny little speck of knowing, it was strong enough to attract better people. And that's when he arrived. Although if you ask any of my friends and loved ones, he definitely wasn't the one I was expecting. I laugh now as I say that because I'm so wildly in love with him. He's not anything that I ever expected, but he is everything that I ever needed.

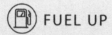 FUEL UP

On the road to self-love, trust that the Universe, God, Source, (pick whatcha like) knows what you need more than you may realize for yourself. Trust that in the unfolding of your life, you will be given what you need to become a better, bolder and more badass version of you. When you step out of the way, you're able to see that what has arrived is really everything you ever needed. So, choose to trust what is.

P.S. I also learned that I *am* really a prize and eventually they do come back. *grin*

Psst–go easy on yourself.

Rest Stop 26

BRIBING GOD

I grew up celebrating only the 'mainstream' Jewish holidays. Specifically, the one that brought me gifts and the other one that guilted me into honoring it or else I might not live another year. But talking specifically about God, we really didn't talk too much about His presence in our lives. God was spoken about as someone who would judge my rights and wrongs, someone from whom I had to seek forgiveness and repentance and someone who would judge how I treated others. And yes, He was spoken about as someone who did love me although that confused me because it felt like He would only love me if I acted a certain way.

Now don't get me wrong. My family didn't mean to make me be fearful of God, but as a young girl that didn't know much about Him, what I witnessed was that my mom seemed to be unhappy and we always seemed to be struggling in some way and so I was uncertain whether God loved us at all or if He just forgot about us. At worst, I wondered if He even existed. So, I did what I do best–I didn't think about it.

It wasn't until many years later when I was heartbroken and lost that I picked up this book, *Conversations with God*, and I felt this tingling inside. I found myself intrigued by this God the author spoke of. The way he described the magic in their relationship made me feel like there might really be something more to this God thing. I felt like the author knew something that I didn't know and had a special relationship with Him that I now thought I wanted. These days you would say that I was experiencing FOMO (Fear Of Missing Out) with God. Something in that book spoke to me and made me feel that maybe God was more than I thought. Maybe I underestimated Him.

Over the years though, as I've looked through my journals, it seems that I was always in search of Him. Always making promises that if He showed up and gave me what I needed, all the ways that I would show up for Him as well. And yes, it sounds like I was trying to bribe God, but I didn't know another way to get Him to show up in ways in which I built Him up to be. So, in each line of my journal, I begged, I pleaded, and I made promises. I promised to do better, to be better, and I even promised to live by His commandments (we watched the movie *The Ten Commandments* every year growing up) if He came into my life and showed Himself to me. I wasn't trying to prove that He was real. I was desperately needing direction and I wanted to hear His voice and His guidance *clearly*. You can't get any clearer than an in-person visit.

My problem had always been a lack of clarity, which then turned into lack of direction. To be honest, I think it was more that I didn't trust my own intuition, or that I was just too scared to listen to it. So, I thought that if it was right in my face, a booming voice or a giant sign or something that made it outside of me, that somehow, I would now listen and follow what it was that God wanted for me.

The truth is that we are always being spoken to, but are we trusting ourselves enough to believe that what we are hearing is that Divine guidance? I was unsure. So, I spent many years ignoring this 'voice' within. I spent many years making opposite choices. And then I spent many years wondering why God wasn't showing up for me and why I had this dark cloud following me. It's funny how we can create a storyline in our minds of how life is when we are the ones writing the script.

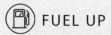 FUEL UP

On the road to self-love, when you choose to trust yourself, then you automatically trust what is being spoken to you. Those signs and loud booming voice that you're seeking, they are right there—smack dab in the stillness and quiet of who you are. Trust yourself.

Psst—go easy on yourself.

Rest Stop 27

GIVE YOURSELF A HUG

When I began my meditation practice, there was a lot that was coming up for me. A lot of emotion, and what felt like places inhabited by a lot of dark shadows. These were places that felt untapped and untouched. Hidden deeply within me was this little girl who longed for protection, safety and security. I began to feel like I was unearthing these feelings the longer I stayed quiet. The longer I allowed myself to not run from what was coming up, the more they emerged. Being in the shower always makes one feel vulnerable and I think that is where she decided to speak to me. While I was bawling my eyes out one day thinking about her and what she needed, I cried aloud, "I just needed a hug!" Then a voice very clearly spoke up and said, "So give yourself a hug."

In my family growing up, we did show affection and would hug each other when we saw one another or left each other. But the hug I really needed was when it was dealing with my sexual abuse. It was nearly impossible for anyone to talk about it, let alone show any affection around it. It was not a topic anyone really wanted to address. We did speak about it, perhaps not in the ways I needed, but we did. But a hug–that was all that seven-year-old needed. So, hearing that message that day in the shower, all those years later, changed everything for me.

I can't go back in time and give her one then, but perhaps this could make up for it now!

So, I closed my eyes and I wrapped my arms around myself so tightly that I could barely let go. The release, the joy, the safety—all of it—it was all mine in that very moment. I cried even more. It has now become my sacred time with me. I look forward to these hugs. I can't begin or end my day without them. I sometimes shower quite a few times a day now.

Try it! It doesn't have to be in the shower if that's a bit weird for you. But just do it. Do it where you feel safe and where you can be every day without fail. You might come to find yourself seeking out these moments like I do.

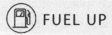 FUEL UP

On the road to self-love, don't be shy about hugging the hell out of yourself. I bet you give some great ones!

P.S. I also use them for guilt when I'm annoyed at my fiancé for not being affectionate enough. I tell him, "Okaaaaay (dramatic pause), I guess I'll just have to go and hug myself again." What? I'm not perfect.

Psst—go easy on yourself.

Rest Stop 28

DON'T FEED THE FUNGUS

She shared very openly with me, "I don't feel good enough in my father's eyes. I feel like nothing I do is good enough for him. He teases me about my weight, asks me all the time when I'm going to get married and always compares me to my older sister who seems to have it all together."

One of my clients has self-worth issues (take a number). When I asked her why she doesn't feel good enough, she stared blankly at me, paused and said, "Because that's what I've been told." I then asked her if anyone has ever praised her. She thought again about it. This time a little bit longer but she came back with a "Yes." I continued, "Okay. Well what is it about your father that makes you choose to believe him over others who have praised you?"

Silence.

"I don't know," she finally said.

Dr. Wayne Dyer once said, "Self-worth cannot be verified by others. You are worthy because you say it is so. If you depend on others for your value, it is other-worth." And who determined that these people who place their judgements and their beliefs on you hold more weight than yours?

Whatever it is that you are holding onto is literally suffocating your awesome. I invite you to think about this. You, my dear one, are holding onto stuff that was never yours from the start. You are carrying around other people's inferiority issues. You're carrying around their insecurities and you're carrying around their hurt. People who hurt people are people in pain.

Deep breath.

I know it doesn't feel good to be a witness to or the target of somebody else's harsh words or judgment. I know what that can do to one's spirit. I grew up thinking that I had to do certain things, act in certain ways and prove myself in order to feel worthy and good enough. I thought I had to measure up to some imaginary bar that I had somehow decided existed. And for the sake of argument, if this bar does exist, at what point in this bar do you have to hit in order to feel good enough? At what point will you be able to look at yourself and say, "Yes, I've arrived"?

I ask this question because as a recovering perfectionist, I have noticed that the bar we set for ourselves keeps getting raised. There is never a 'perfect' and there will never be a 'good enough'. It's up to you to be ready to toss this fabricated idea that there is anything or anybody else that you need to be in order to be your amazing self.

So, are you done with the B.S.? Or is this something you enjoy carrying around? And I'm genuinely not trying to be a smart ass (although it's sometimes hard to tell with me). At some point in your life, if you are truly wanting to finally feel good in your skin and finally live a life that feels good, then you have to be willing to cut the cord with these beliefs that you have picked up along the way. They are simply someone else's bullshit.

Let me repeat for emphasis (and change it into first person). Feel free to say this aloud: *I am willing to cut the cord with these beliefs that I have picked up that simply are someone else's bullshit. I choose to not be weighed down by what isn't mine.*

You might be wondering–why do we carry this around? Little kids are sponges. We want to be good in our parents' eyes, smart in our teachers' eyes and cool in our friends' eyes. But nobody has ever told us that we don't have to do any of this. So, we spend our time trying to measure up, to impress and to be everything except who we genuinely are. And so when somebody in your life who you look up to says or does something that makes you think that you're not doing the job (being cool or whatever that is for you) you think you're supposed to be doing, you take it to heart. You may feel as if you've now disappointed someone, or let them down, or just couldn't measure up to the standards you thought they set for you. And this sense of letdown becomes implanted deep within you.

Over the years you feed this feeling of disappointing others with other experiences that have made you feel the same way and this belief grows and grows (like a fungus) until it feels like an extension of you. This fungus shows up as limiting beliefs, toxic thought patterns and self-sabotaging behavior. The one thing that you must do in order to separate yourself from this fungus (that isn't yours) is the willingness to recognize that it isn't yours. So, how do you do that? You get to know yourself by spending time with yourself.

By the way, you know what's funny? When I decided to have some heart-to-heart conversations with those whose crap I was carrying around from something they either said or did–they never even remembered saying it or doing it in the first place. Seriously! Ask them. Here you and I are carrying around some heavy-duty pain and holding it deeply within, letting some nasty fungus grow and these people don't even remember saying it or if they do, they didn't actually mean it the way we heard it. Ha! What a complete waste of friggin' time. I don't know about you, but I certainly am tired of dragging that mess around.

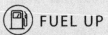 FUEL UP

On the road to self-love, get to know yourself. Spend time with those who really see your greatness. Put other people's opinions in perspective and get to living a life not based on others' standards but based on what feels good in that crazy, magnificent soul of yours!

Psst—go easy on yourself.

Rest Stop 29

RUNNING FROM THE INSIDE

I waited until it got late, and I knew everyone was settled down for the evening in their dorm rooms, except for the other night owls who were working late or like me, sneaking off to eat. I didn't plan it. Most nights my intention was to settle in like everyone else but as soon as things got quiet outside, the inside of me started getting rowdy.

Whoppers–they were the chosen distraction. These were my numbing mechanism. They were my comfort. It's not that I didn't want to face or feel my emotions; it's just that I didn't realize that I wasn't. All I knew was that it didn't feel good to think about certain things, so I just didn't think about them. I wasn't consciously trying to avoid or distract; I just did what felt better. And at that time, a Whopper and fries did.

Now of course, what didn't feel better was watching myself grow out of everything, or the terror I felt when it was weigh-in day at school and they would announce your weight out loud through what seemed like a megaphone to me; or the anxiety I felt when we approached the weigh-in station for oversized vehicles on the highways and I would cry because I thought it was for humans. But in the moment, that high I got from ordering food and sitting down and eating it—that made the pain go away.

If you're like me, it's not that you're choosing to run or distract; you're just choosing to not hurt. I mean, why would anyone choose to want to consciously feel badly? On top of that, I had spent a good portion of my formative years being told how strong I was, so I definitely would not be caught running from anything.

When you've been let down, disappointed, betrayed and abandoned, that leaves a pretty massive scar. It sometimes can feel like a gaping hole that never can be filled and so even trying is too painful. So, you turn away. You close off. You don't leave yourself open to be hurt that way again.

This shutting down is simply your heart's way of trying to protect itself. It's not meaning any harm. It just wants to not have to feel that way ever again. But within that isolation, lies a deep hurt—a wounded child that simply needs love, attention and for me, a hug.

I understand *why* you've protected yourself. I know the reasons *why* you've not let people in, or let the wrong people in and mostly, haven't let yourself in. I know *why* you often feel so alone even in the midst of people around you who might love you to pieces. I know *why* you might still feel incomplete, discontent and unhappy even when everything on paper says you have it all.

Gorgeous being, I promise that you'll be okay. I assure you that when you put away your distractions, and turn *towards* instead of away from, choose to feel compassion instead of shame and choose to feel kindness instead of anger, you will begin to heal. Mostly, you will begin to find the (self) love and happiness you are seeking.

 FUEL UP

On the road to self-love, allow yourself to feel again. It's time to re-visit what you have left behind. It's time to reopen that place you've turned away from. But this time, it's time to do it with love.

Psst–go easy on yourself.

Rest Stop 30

LIFE & DEATH

It was all so heavy. Everything was so life and death. The guy who didn't call me when he said he would. The nights I stayed up crying wondering what was wrong with me. What did I do wrong? Why wasn't I good enough for him? If you asked me now who these guys were that had me doubting my worth, I wouldn't be able to give you a name. I can barely remember their faces. Yup, it was, I was, so dramatic.

Now I'm not diminishing what I went through. I'm just saying that maybe something you're going through right now might not matter in a few years. Perhaps you won't even be able to remember it.

Maybe a lot of what you go through isn't meant to make you suffer but rather to learn, experience and grow. Maybe what you're going through is meant to help you figure out what you want and how you feel. What if you didn't have to be controlled by your emotions? What if I could've simply understood at the time that it was no reflection on me and that there was simply someone else out there for me and we would meet at the right time?

Maybe, just maybe, the deeper understanding of the bigger picture can assist you as you navigate through life. Maybe everything doesn't have to be so hard or so dramatic but just experiences as we move through life. Easier said than done? Maybe, if you're not ready for it. But I can tell you this—as soon as I decided not to take everything so personally and to truly trust in what was happening, the unreturned phone calls suddenly became blessings as I knew it was just one more person who was leading me closer to MY person.

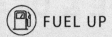 **FUEL UP**

On the road to self-love, remember that you and only you determine how important something is and you and only you choose how you will feel about it. Life and death simply should be reserved for true life and death situations.

Psst—go easy on yourself.

Rest Stop 31

TELL FEAR YOU GOT THIS COVERED

I've always been an overachiever. Whether it was me in school always being done first with my test and running up to the teachers desk to turn it in, being awarded 'Employee of the Month' at a temp job or even being that 1% that has the most unusual complications to some medical procedure, there has always been something in me that just doesn't know how to do something half-ass. It's one of the reasons sitting down and writing this book has been a full-time avoidance job. It's that part of me that needs it to be perfect. It's the part of me that can't take a risk that it might not turn out as great as I think it should be.

I'm honestly sitting here writing this right now because my head is tired of hearing the nagging from my soul telling me to shut the f*** up and just write—perfect or not. This nagging also led me to my spiritual path. This nagging led me to take off on a ninety-day solo adventure to Italy and this nagging is ultimately what led me to see me and fall in love with me. This 'nagging' is simply your voice—your spirit, your essence, your truth. Whatever you want to call it, it's your guide and it will always lead you in the right direction. It will never, ever betray or abandon you. The only thing you and I need to do is step aside and take our hands off the steering wheel.

The voice within is *your* inner wisdom. We all have it. You do, too. Sometimes that voice is drowned out by the other voice–the one that lives in your mind and is born through fear. I'm not speaking about the voice from your mind. I'm talking about the one that is light filled. I'm talking about the one that is born of and speaks through your soul. This is the voice that keeps you going, even when things don't seem to make a lick of sense and every 'common sense' thing points towards saying "No", this voice pushes you forward.

"You can do this."
"You're meant for more than this."
"You're a star."
"You are special."

These thoughts reverberated in my head throughout my life but mostly when I was younger. Through all the fighting, the challenges, the broken hearts and letdowns, these words and mainly feelings kept pushing me forward–even when everyone told me to have a plan B or to get my head out of the clouds.

⛽ FUEL UP

On the road to self-love, choose to pay attention to the voice of love–the one that reminds you of your magnificence and potential, the one that speaks your truths, cheers you on and encourages you to show up. Acknowledge your fearful voice that speaks up, too, as it's just wanting your attention. Tell fear you appreciate its concern for you, but you and love have got this handled.

Psst–go easy on yourself.

Rest Stop 32

STEP AWAY FROM THE BAG OF CHIPS

Quite a few years ago, my mom came to me and told me that she had found Jesus. Now that might not sound strange to you except that we're Jewish. It literally felt like she woke up one day, rolled over and decided to tell me everything that we had ever been taught was now no longer true. While it could have very easily rocked my world, I was searching so badly at the time for answers to everything, especially the pain I was in, that you could've told me Dr. Seuss was now our Lord and Savior and I would've jumped on the bandwagon!

At that time of the Jesus announcement, I had spent about fifteen years reading the self-help section of the bookstores, going to self-help workshops, watching and listening to anyone who could just ease something within me. I took on all their advice -positive affirmations, journaling, mirror exercises, meditation, writing forgiveness letters, chanting. I mean you name it; I was doing it. While all these work, when you have no idea what it is you are truly seeking except just to not be unhappy, it can become overwhelmingly depressing and confusing.

So, when my Mom came to me with Jesus being the answer, I did what anyone would do who wanted so desperately to feel good: I started praying to Him. I wrote to Him in my journal and made promises and declarations and announcements that I would do anything He wanted if He would just make me happy! Every day and every moment, I waited. I waited for something to shift. I waited for some part of me to feel better. And some days I did feel better!

My journal pages were filled with revelations, inspiration and positivity! There were some moments of complete surrender and faith. There were other moments of true understanding. And then, there were the down times. I would turn the journal page and the next entry would be how pathetic I was and how I was thinking about *insert any guy's name* that was treating me like crap again or how I was eating like crap again.

"Step away from the bag of chips." I've always felt like I needed someone to say that to me while I was in full attack mode. And I don't mean regarding the numerous bags of chips. I mean regarding me. I was so lost and not wanting to face what needed to be faced, that I often found my face buried in food. But as you guessed it, the answers weren't found at the bottom of that bag either. Jesus didn't provide the answers. The empty Whopper wrappers didn't provide the answers. Nothing seemed to make things better except this one thing.

There was this energy that seemed to keep pulling me up. This light of sorts, not super bright that I could see. It was guiding me and leading me away from all this pain. Up and out. Some energy, some force that told me there was more for me than this life I was currently living. I heard this voice that intuitively knew that life was supposed to feel better than this; that I was supposed to feel better than this. And the only thing I knew to do was to keep paying attention and begin to make choices that felt good.

I was exhausted from this self-abuse. I literally used to see the brick wall that I was heading right towards and instead of slowing down, I would press harder on the gas pedal. I was tired of so much seeking. I was done.

I realized that I felt better when I didn't eat an entire bag of chips. I realized that I felt better when I didn't go out with a guy that I knew wasn't good for me. I realized I felt better when I showed up for an audition instead of going out with friends. I suddenly began to take notice of what *good* felt like and I realized I wanted more of *that*!

Sometimes being happy isn't about making all these difficult changes in your life or even trying to figure it all out. It's simply about checking in with yourself and noticing what feels good and what doesn't. So, the good news is that if you're feeling overwhelmed about where you are in your life and all the changes you feel you need to make, you don't have to go changing your entire way of being. You just need to take notice of what doesn't feel good and then no longer do that. Figure out what *does* feel good and then do more of *that*.

I can very confidently tell you this: it doesn't lie in the empty pizza box or in the bottom of a six-pack or even in the fourth time you've worked out that day. It's never been about anyone or anything else. It's always been you. That light you seek, that contentment and completion, that perfection and blinding light is you and you don't have to search high and low for it. You see, you already are it and once you realize that, you just have to slightly shift back to center and plug back in.

I know. I know. It seems like I'm oversimplifying what currently might feel like anything but easy. But I can assure you I'm not. It just seems that way because you've become so enmeshed and led by your mind that you have attached your being-ness to it. You have given your power over to it being something else that you need in order to be happy and you've forgotten the magic and wonder of your soul. This, my dear friend, is what you will return to–your home, your magic, your *you*.

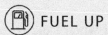

FUEL UP

On the road to self-love, take a deep breath, beautiful soul, and know that in all of this that might seem overwhelming, lies a simplicity that will have you nod your head in amusement as it was simply a puzzle piece that needed to be moved ever so slightly back into place.

Psst–go easy on yourself.

Rest Stop 33

S.O.S.– SHINY OBJECT SYNDROME

I'll be happy when I get a different job.

I'll be happy when I lose weight.

I'll be happy when I pay off my bills, get a boyfriend, have money, etc.

I remember thinking that my entire life would change once I lost weight. I would finally like myself and I would finally be happy. And then once I did that, I would obviously make better choices in the men I dated because I would be feeling so good about myself. I would never allow anyone to mistreat or disrespect this hot and confident girl. Yes! Being skinny would change everything!

So, I lost over 100 pounds. I bought a brand-new wardrobe. I updated all my online dating pics. I started going on more auditions. And guess what? I was still dating shitty men, still treated myself poorly, and I still didn't like myself any more than I did before. WTF! Okay, I really did like my new wardrobe, but even that got old after a while because some other 'shiny thing' came along that convinced me that 'it' was what I needed to be happy.

S.O.S.

We all have it: Shiny Object Syndrome. It's that thing that looks so good and you think it will solve everything for you, so you continue to chase it, whatever it is. It has convinced you that once you achieve it, get it, obtain it, change it–you will be happy! Does this sound familiar? The "I'll be happy when" disease. Always *something* that you need in order to be happy.

Here's the thing about these shiny objects–there will *always* be something shinier! There will always be something that you feel that you need to make you feel better. This is ultimately what *Loving Yourself Happy* is about. If you don't figure out how to be happy, content and filled with joy right now in *this* very moment–even if it feels sucky, then you will never find it even when all your *fill in the blanks* get achieved.

Figure out who the hell you are without all the external stuff. Write a list of all the great things you love about yourself. List your strengths, your rockstar capabilities and abilities. Sit with exactly who you are right now and look yourself in the mirror and realize that the only shiny thing you will ever need is staring back at you.

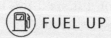 **FUEL UP**

On the road to self-love, stop looking elsewhere for everything you think you need. SHINE ON like the glitter bomb that you already are!

Psst–go easy on yourself.

Rest Stop 34

STOP APOLOGIZING

"Oh, I'm so sorry! I didn't mean to be so needy. I just thought that when you liked someone that you made more time for them. It's been three days since I've heard from you. You had said you were really sick, so when I heard you were out at the bars, that made me mad. Sorry. I know we are just friends. I know. Sorry."

Seriously! What the hell was *I* apologizing for? For speaking up? For stating my needs? For being rightfully upset? Yup, all of it. I was the queen of apologizing for my feelings, for apologizing for speaking my truth and saying what was on my mind and in my heart. I apologized for possibly, just maybe having ruffled some feathers and I apologized for just being. I shared how I truly felt (wrapped in a joke), and then quickly responded with "just kidding" or "I'm sorry!"

Stop apologizing! I know I might seem angry but I'm NOT going to apologize for it or anything, for that matter! And you better get used to it! Oh, sorry. I hope I didn't offend you.

Is this you? Phew. Good–then it was just me. I was so afraid that someone wouldn't like me, or I would lose someone if I said something wrong, that I lost my own voice along the way. Until this day…

I am ready to stop apologizing for who I am and what I feel.

(5/11/2003 journal entry)

I am not sure what had shifted that day, maybe something I drank, but that was the day I was done not being able to own my truth. That was the day that I was done trying to worry about everyone else's feelings while ignoring my own. That was it. When you spend a lifetime walking on eggshells, eventually they are going to break. No matter how careful you try to be to not hurt someone or even gently rock the boat, someone along the way will misinterpret what you say and there isn't a damn thing you will be able to do about it. So, I was done being apologetic for something I wasn't sorry for.

For clarity sake, I'm not talking about being disrespectful or rude to someone. I'm talking about just speaking up about the way that you feel about a situation, towards something or someone. I'm talking about just voicing *you*. Standing in and owning your truth.

What I discovered is that in speaking my truth, I no longer felt the need to apologize because it felt so damn good to actually be forming words that sounded like what I was *really* thinking and what I was *really* wanting to say. So no, I'm not sorry for what I said or for my being. And if my *light* bothers you, I have a pair of sunglasses you're welcome to borrow.

 FUEL UP

On the road to self-love, only use the words 'I'm sorry' when you've hurt someone.

Psst—go easy on yourself.

Rest Stop 35

STOP COMPARING YOURSELF

I am guilty of being jealous of others' successes. There I said it. I sometimes look at these famous inspirational speakers and wonder what they have that I don't. Why are they standing on stages in front of thousands of people and sharing a message like I do, and yet here I am sitting behind my computer watching *them*?

I'm a motivational speaker, self-love and joy coach and I run an entire wellness community. I inspire and help people to love themselves and to live their best life. So, why the hell do I still deal with some of this un-evolved and un-enlightened nonsense? Because I'm human. Because I still face the same shit that you do. I am not immune to 'occasional' tantrums, to lashing out, to sabotaging myself, to not always making the best choices and any of the other human fallacies we all have, including jealousy.

The really cool thing about this, however, is that I have learned tools to be able to navigate my way through my impulsive behaviors and feelings that sometimes rear their annoying head. I have become aware of what I do and why I do it, and I don't punish myself because of it. And because of the gentle way that I treat myself, I have found myself being less reactionary, and ultimately not making the same choices I used to. You might be wondering what does that look like? It looks like me not being angry at someone and wishing them failure simply because I'm jealous of their success. (Don't judge. I never said the truth was pretty.)

Beautiful soul, I beg of you, stop comparing yourself to the person you see online or in the media or anyone that you think has this amazing life and wonder why you aren't as successful and happy as them. My friend just recently told me how happy he is. He lit up as he shared that with me. He loves what he is doing. He loves his job and his life. And I sat there listening to him and wondered why I didn't feel the same way. What secret sauce did he have that I wasn't given?

And what I know to be absolutely true and reminded myself of later when I got home and slapped some sense into myself is that we each have our own path to walk. What very well may make someone else happy, may not make me happy. There might be areas in his life that he wishes were more like areas in my life. So, playing this comparison game with others' lives, especially on social media, where everyone's highlight reel is in your face–it's a waste of freaking time. Your life isn't supposed to look like somebody else's. You're here to rock what you've got and trying to be anything other than you, only has you show up as a half-baked, inauthentic you. And that is boring.

Please don't think I don't understand how hard it is to look at someone and see them have what you want and wonder why you don't or can't also have it. It's not your job to figure out why somebody else has something you want. It's your job to go and create the life *you* want.

⛽ FUEL UP

On the road to self-love, remember–there is only one of you and any time you spend trying to be somebody other than you, you are literally robbing the world of your greatness. Go on a self-archaeo-logical dig because what you will unearth will be awe-inspiring. It's the reason you were born.

Psst–go easy on yourself.

Rest Stop 36

ALL ROADS LEAD HOME

I've always taken the long way around—the long and winding road to be more specific. No matter if it was in the love department, figuring out my career or finally getting my health on point, I seem to always take the scenic route. While there are others who like to get from point A to B in record time, I am an explorer when it comes to journeying through my life. And, to be quite honest, it drives some people in my life crazy! But there's good news here! There is no right or wrong route. There isn't only one path to travel down.

Like most people these days, when you're driving somewhere you aren't familiar with, you probably use your GPS. You enter the address of your destination and you're given a choice of a few different routes. One route is more direct, but perhaps with a bit more traffic. Another route has less miles but with some tolls. While each one of these routes has their own challenges, the two commonalities they all have is that all of them have an arrival time and they all lead to the same destination.

When it comes to your life, the one thing I implore you to keep in mind is this: you are not on the wrong path. You are headed in the right direction. Just keep in mind, there might be an *easier* route.

As you go about living your life, no matter what path you choose to go down, no matter what challenges you come across and no matter what setbacks you might encounter, ultimately you always end up at your destination. The decision is yours in *how* you want to get there.

You can be the person who packs your car up with a bunch of screaming banshees, blaring the most aggravating music while criticizing and judging your driving; or you can be the person who chooses someone you love to journey with while listening to the best music, feeling the wind in your hair while you're taking the stunning scenic route. The quality of your journey is up to you.

I'm not going to lie. No matter how prepared you think you are for the journey, there will always be unexpected things that happen along the way. That's life, my friend. And that's what makes it so unbelievably perfect! And no, I didn't always feel this way.

I have gone on some crazy-ass adventures to get to this place where I can look in the mirror and feel love and respect for who I see and for who I am. And it didn't come with sheltering myself off from the world, or being angry at the world, or even thinking that I knew it all. Self-love, self-respect and ultimately my happiness came from my insatiable appetite for wanting to better myself. It comes from my passionate desire to always want to know more, learn more and grow into a better or even best version of me. I may never learn 'the' reason why I am actually here. I may never figure it all out, but while I'm here, I certainly am going to make this one hell of a ride!

THAT is the route I have chosen to take on this journey.

⛽ FUEL UP

On the road to self-love, there might be some detours and construction along the way, perhaps some traffic and potholes. If you equip yourself for the journey with the things that make it easier, then you're much more capable of handling the unexpected along the way. As these challenges in life arise, be prepared for them and always know that you will end up exactly where you intended to be (or somewhere better!).

Psst—go easy on yourself.

Rest Stop 37

SELF-WORTH CAN BE
A STICKY SUBJECT

"Come on, Shari.
You can do this.
Pick your head up and look at me.
We are walking away now.
We can't do this anymore.
I promise you that I will take care of you."

I don't know how many times I told myself, "*Never again, Shari.*" So many times, I guess that it just became like a well-rehearsed play and I just wanted to keep trying out my acting skills to see how many different ways I could say it. I'm making light of this right now, but it was unbelievably exhausting. It's a roller coaster ride you take yourself on. Right when you've pulled back into the station and you have the opportunity to hop off, you choose to sit there and take another ride. Seriously! You sit there and watch yourself in slow motion pull away and slowly creep up that ol' crickety, loud, rattling track that is about to start knocking you around all over again. Yeah, dumb. I know.

I finally understood that I was the one creating this mess after some proverbial bruises and broken bones–that and a truly soul-humiliating, rock-bottom moment covered in a McDonald's strawberry milkshake dripping down from the top of my head. Yes, I had had enough. Well, I stormed off having "had enough." I was done. That was it! I was better than this and I knew it. I knew it so deep within my soul that I felt like I literally could hear the screams bellowing from deep within. They were just begging me to really be done this time.

I believed it. I really did. Somewhere inside I knew that this was it, but I just didn't know how to stop. I didn't know how to walk away thinking that someone didn't love me or think that I was good enough for them. I just had to be sure the person knew that I was good enough; so, I found myself standing back at their door, remnants of sticky strawberry shake on me, trying to convince him how worthy I was of being taken care of, loved and respected. And all the while I was saying these things to him, inside I was screaming them to myself.

I felt like I was having a true out-of-body experience. I could see myself so clearly standing in front of his door, demanding to be respected. Yet there I stood completely begging somebody who just threw a drink in my face to see me and love me. It wasn't my finest moment. But there was *somebody* who heard that message loud and clear.

Me.

I'd like to tell you that I had the courage to walk away when I was finished with my pity monologue. However, that would just be an outright lie. He told me to come inside and we had sex later that night. As I laid there, feeling complete shame, I knew I had really had enough. I drove away in the middle of the night and never picked up a phone call, answered a text or ever had communication with him ever again.

As in any journey, there are ups and downs and twists and turns. I'd also love to tell you that I never made a poor decision again. I'd love to tell you that I never chose another man to love (or obsess over) that didn't love me back. But again, that would be a lie. The truth is, though, I *did* feel different. Something in me *did* shift that day. I saw clearly where I wanted to go, and I wasn't busy looking back at where I had been. I was focused and determined and like anyone who wants to get somewhere, you keep moving forward. Yes, you might even take the long and scenic road around, but you are certain that you will end up at your destination.

And so, that's what I worked towards. That's what I was guided by every day. Yeah, cute smiles got me off track some days, but I always found my way back. I knew what self-respect and self-worth tasted like and I didn't want to ever give that up!

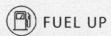 FUEL UP

On the road to self-love, you will come face to face with people and things who will make you question yourself, your integrity and your worth. The good news is that none of those people or things can determine that for you. You may not know what it feels like right now, but once you gift yourself with a moment where you stand up for yourself and stick to something that you know is right for you, you will forever remember that feeling and you will never want to undervalue or diminish yourself ever again.

Psst–go easy on yourself.

Rest Stop 38

RELEASING BAGGAGE

"You're better off without them."

"They'll realize their loss."

"They don't matter."

These are the things that were said to me every single time somebody left me, every time someone broke my heart, forgot about me or made me feel unworthy and unimportant.

Imagine losing a lifelong friendship? Now imagine losing another one within the same year. And then another one. That's some heart-freak-ing-breaking stuff to handle. Talk about a whole range of emotions and some real self-reflection going on. And with that self-reflection comes a lot of confusion, pain, self-doubt, anger, more anger, sadness, and sorrow. I know this because it happened to me.

I was growing. What seemed to be happening is that my circle of friends that I had since college was also growing, but just in a different direction. I didn't understand it because to me, true friendships are supposed to be unconditional. You support the people you love on the journeys they take even if they veer off from what you're doing. But that isn't what happened, not in any of those cases. Each one had their own reason to stop speaking to me; and each one hurt really deeply in their own way.

It's hard to come to terms with things like this. Unexpected losses of *any* kind–job, relationship, friendship, etc. – these are not easy to cope with when you feel dumped. It's not easy when you feel dispensable and unimportant to somebody. Feeling like this has been a really tough thing that I have dealt with throughout my life, especially with men.

I spent so much time suffering over why I wasn't important enough for them to stick around. I heard those encouraging words bellowing in my head from my loved ones telling me that I'm better off without them or they just were selfish or whatever platitude they offered to try to make me feel better. But all I could see was me alone and not being good enough. No matter what anybody said, I just couldn't make sense of it or find peace with it. If I was worthy and good enough then they would see it and they still would be here with me. I called bullshit on it, so I completely feel you right now. There is nothing that I could say to you at this moment that might change your mind if you are currently in this place.

One of the things, however, that began helping to ease this uncomfortable feeling within was recognizing other instances in my life where things didn't go the way I had hoped. Looking back, I was able to see that I was actually better off without them or without that thing. I saw how different opportunities arose in my life. Different people showed up. I uncovered and discovered parts of myself that I didn't know existed and that I liked! By trusting in this release process, I created space for my new life to bloom.

- for me to bloom!

I learned to rely and trust myself. I found that I always seemed to be the one that was there for me and that in itself had me fall more in love with me. This meant I no longer had to hold on to others for dear life. And more importantly, I didn't have to doubt myself or my worth because they chose to not stick around. And with that, I found I no longer *needed* anyone else.

Now this doesn't mean that I don't enjoy people or desire their company. What it means is that I am no longer dependent on anyone to make me feel whole and complete. I never feel that there is anything wrong with me simply because something or somebody was gone.

The thing is, life never came with a handbook that said things would be easy. It never said you and I wouldn't feel pain and shit wouldn't be hard. But in every challenge that we go through, we expand. We become our better parts. We remember the truth of who we are even if it means walking through some heavy mud to get there. Just like in nature, there are seasons when we must release and not fight it. Whether it's someone walking away, an opportunity that you've lost, or making the choice that it's time for you to go.

 FUEL UP

On the road to self-love, you might lose some people along the way. Don't allow this to distract or detract you from your journey. This road will be painful, but your journey will also become lighter and allow for more space, healing and blessings that you didn't have room for before. Some will return and others won't and the best thing you can do is thank them for their presence in your life, for feeding your spirit at the time you needed it most and then wish them well along their continued journey.

Psst–go easy on yourself.

Rest Stop 39

NOT ALL WHO
WANDER ARE LOST

I've never been the shortcut kind of girl. There are times I would have loved to have gotten to where I wanted (or desperately needed) to go more quickly and gracefully. In coming to understand who I am and later into the full acceptance of who I am, I'm a wanderer, a traveler, an explorer.

When I was two years old, my mom started sending me and my older sister from Florida to New York to spend the summers with my grand-parents. I fell in love with the tray tables, the food, my wing pin, the fluffy clouds, the kids' activity pack, and the stewardesses who would sit and play with us. I fell in love with everything about traveling. The romanticism of staring out the airplane, car or train windows, any window that I was able to watch the world go by as I was heading somewhere. My soul just loved to explore.

For me, sitting still begins to make me feel enclosed and I can often find myself holding my breath. I become uncomfortable in my own skin. I get antsy. The moment I jump into my car to go somewhere, I exhale. (I've also been known to scream YEEEEEEHAW, but that's only when I'm going on a long trip. You probably noticed it when we started this road trip together.)

So, after those summers in New York, I tried to find any way to travel. I couldn't wait to go away to college. Right after high school graduation, I packed up and moved from Miami to Syracuse, New York for college! I then packed up for a semester and moved to London, England. After college graduation, I packed up and moved from Syracuse down to New York City. After some years there, I packed up and moved out west to Los Angeles, then to Italy for a few months, then back to New York City and then back to Los Angeles.

People began questioning whether I was running from something and inherently I knew—*no*! I wasn't running *from* something. I was running *to* everything! To see! To explore! To feel! To grow! To smile! I am a wanderer in life. My spirit still lights up at the thought of even just getting behind that wheel and fully feeling all that life has to offer out there on the open road and wide, expansive places.

Along these wanderings is where I grow. It's where my life takes me on roundabouts and detours. It reminds me to slow down and take a rest at the next exit. With that good rest comes a refueling and reenergizing. My big and bold life has been experienced fully by wandering, by saying, "Yes" even when I'm scared and by continuing to get up even after falling. I have experienced my life fully by the glimmer of hope and sparkle that remains in my eyes as I travel this road.

FUEL UP

On the road to self-love, if you also find yourself wandering, embrace it. There is so much to see and experience in the world. Open your eyes and heart to all that is out there. See life through the eyes of curiosity and give yourself permission to explore. What you find will open you up in ways you never knew possible and will get you one mile marker closer back to you.

Psst—go easy on yourself.

Rest Stop 40

"ARE YOU HAPPY"

"Are you happy, Shari?"

Holy crap. I sat across the table with a big pizza pie between the two of us and these four words slowly spilled out of his mouth. Each word felt like a dagger.

Pause.
Bigger pause.
Excruciatingly long pause.

"Uhhh…Sometimes?"

Shit! This question in this moment really just f*cked shit up for me. I mean, I had thought about this before. Okay, I had thought about it often. I knew I wasn't jumping for joy every day when I woke up, but really, are there people that do? I used to jump for joy, but now that I think about it, that might've been a superficial leap.

There is this part of me that I knew felt incomplete and that something was missing, but to say the actual words, "I am not happy" threw me for a f*cking loop. And I'm sorry, Mom, about this language but I don't know another way to express my dumbfoundedness, shock, and general disf*cking belief. I mean how could a joy coach and motivational speaker *not* be happy?

I'm still working on that answer but the one thing that I do know is that I am loving myself through this disbelief. I am being gentle with myself and trying to understand where this feeling of unhappiness comes from and not beat myself up over it and judge myself because of it. Because that is just a whole other pile of shit I do not need on top of why am I not happy.

Side note: We often suffer more in life because of the judgment we place on ourselves and situations rather than the circumstances themselves. So, I certainly wasn't going to pile on unnecessary weight on my already fragile self.

While I wanted to shove another slice of pizza in my mouth and completely ignore the question, instead I opened up. I shared how I felt there was a part of me that wasn't living my purpose. And for me, that makes me feel disconnected, discontent and ultimately not happy. My saving grace is that I know that this thing we call happiness is all temporary. It's based on external things. Joy is what is steadfast and secure. It sits in your soul. It is who we are and what we are made of. Joy is never changing.

Although this unhappiness question threw my ass off my seat, what I do know is that I can create a life that feels better and more connected and ultimately happier. This isn't a death sentence but rather a gift that I've been given to show me that I am living slightly out of center and all I have to do is find my way back.

FUEL UP

On the road to self-love, if there is a part of you that isn't feeling happy, I invite you to find your way back to center. Love yourself through it. See the blessing wrapped in the message. And then pick your jaw up off the f*cking floor and get to living a blissfully happy life! And the times that it doesn't feel that way, say thank you for the guidance and give yourself a hug.

P.S. Two days later I was happy again. See? It's all temporary so don't go investing your energy into worry.

Psst—go easy on yourself.

Rest Stop 41

IT'S OKAY TO FEEL ANGER

Today I said F*CK YOU to the man who abused me.

For many years I spoke about him and his illness. I saw his innocence and his hurt. I felt for him. While I knew that what he did was wrong, I couldn't find the anger within me.

But today I said F*CK YOU.

F*CK YOU for choosing a little girl to take advantage of.
F*CK YOU for taking my innocence.
F*CK YOU for threatening my family in exchange for my silence.
F*CK YOU for making me think all these years that I wasn't important enough to protect.
And F*CK YOU for making me think that I must walk through this world not making mistakes so I wouldn't get hurt again.

Today I said f*ck you to him and I LOVE YOU to me.

 FUEL UP

On the road to self-love, sometimes unexpected anger will come up out of nowhere. This will help you heal mountains of pain you didn't know you were carrying. Love yourself (and hug yourself) through it.

Psst—go easy on yourself.

Rest Stop 42

LIGHTEN UP

Some days, you just gotta rock out with your hairbrush in the mirror!

Some days, you gotta put on your sexy, shimmery tights and French-cut leotard and dance like you're a Solid Gold dancer! (That's for all you 80's babies.)

Some days, you gotta just sit and do nothing–no stinkin' thinkin, no obsessing, complaining or worrying–nada, zip, zilch, nothing.

Some days, you just gotta walk into a room and exclaim, "I am a mother f'n badass!" and then flip your hair and walk out of the room!

Some days, you just gotta ditch all this heavy bullshit and enjoy every ounce of your life. Life really is a lot easier and simpler than we often make it.

Some days, you just gotta take a look at all that I wrote in this book and ditch it! One day it will all come together for you and you'll smile at the absurdity of it all.
(Oh great, now I tell you this after you've read it all)

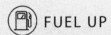 FUEL UP

On the road to self-love, stop waiting until the end to receive your prize. Your prize are the moments of your life. The ordinary things that you often don't pay attention to. String those together and that's what makes your life extraordinary. Ditch the heavy load and lighten up!

Psst—go easy on yourself.

Detour

THE REUNION

It's interesting the things that have to happen in our lives that finally make us follow through on a lifelong dream or goal. One only hopes that our own strong desire for it will be enough to bring us to this point, but that isn't always the case. If you're anything like me, it's usually something that has come and knocked you on your ass and finally made you take action. This can come in the form of a divorce, getting cheated on, a major illness, losing your job, and really any other unexpected devastating blow. For me, it was a breakup.

I had been dating this new guy, John, for a few years on and off (long distance relationship) and we had finally made a big decision (and commitment) that he was going to move from New York to Los Angeles for us to be together. Now, for us to have gotten to this point was a *huge* deal. I mean, I had to go through my own shit to realize that I was deserving of the love he was laying on me and it took me quite a few years to finally let down those walls I had built up since my earlier heartbreak. He always said that the 2x4 he had been hitting me over the head with finally wore me down. He was right. I had given my heart over and said *"yes"* to a full-time relationship and a full-time, filled-up heart!

I told my roommate that he and I were going to move in together and so she began looking for her own place. All was in motion and things were going swimmingly–until he decided that it was all a bit too scary and he just wasn't ready.

Record scratch!

Excuse my language, but WTF! You're not ready?? You've been chasing me for close to five years and I finally give my heart over and *you* are scared? It felt like me and especially my heart had been thrown out to sea, left floating out there all alone and nobody could hear my screams.

So, this decision of his to not come to Los Angeles ultimately began the breakdown of our relationship. Other things came up, too–his fears about me, my intentions towards him, etc. It was truly a shit show. We called it quits.

Now when something this big happens to us, we are left with two choices. Either we sit in our misery or we get our asses up and go do something crazy! And considering you're on this road trip with me, my crazy showed up as deciding to take off to Italy by myself for the entire summer.

There's nothing quite like mending a broken heart by going off to an-other country that just happens to have the hottest men in the world. Okay, that's not 100% true. I honestly had no interest in the hot men at that moment (but I reserve the right to change my mind). I only had my eyes set on writing the book I had been dreaming about, sitting on sidewalk cafes drinking my doppio espressos, sipping wine and de-vouring salami, cheese and fresh baguettes (in any order all day long). Since I had nowhere to live and no reason to be in L.A., this made perfect sense! So, I quit my job of fourteen years, sold my car and all my furniture, and put what personal items were left in a 5x5 storage unit and off I went. I traveled with my broken heart in tow but with my big dreams leading the way.

Arriverderci, Los Angeles! Ciao, Italy!

Four months later, I found myself on an airplane to a small little village in the Tuscan countryside ready to write and heal (credit goes to the movie *Under the Tuscan Sun* for this decision making). I even dubbed this adventure 'Heal, Write, Love' (credit goes to Elizabeth Gilbert for this decision making). I chose this quaint, tiny town because I wanted to be with myself. I wanted to go on a solo adventure. Truthfully, I just wanted to be as far away from people as possible and the idea of rolling hills, endless bottles of wine, train rides and sidewalk cafes to write my memoir seemed to breathe through my every thought, so I just went with it!

What followed that summer was nothing like the movie I had envisioned; yet everything that it was supposed to be. Often in our lives, we go with all these expectations and wants and what shows up is usually everything but that.

I didn't write the book I was intending to. I didn't enjoy being alone all the time. And I didn't stop thinking about him. As a matter of fact, we kept in touch that summer, but that's another story for another time.

There were moments of complete and total loneliness. There were moments of doubt about myself and what the hell I was doing there. There were days of complete boredom with nothing to do but watch ant assembly lines. But what I came to find out was that loneliness, self-doubt and those ants were everything that I needed to experience.

You see, I had spent my entire life being surrounded by people. Filling my days and nights with parties and distractions and going. I never had an opportunity to sit with myself and with my feelings and to just be with *me*. I had spent so many years running from my truth and myself that this complete cut off from even knowing the language and having anyone to communicate with forced me to sit deeper with myself. Sitting and watching those ants was an opportunity for me to be fully present, to get out of my head, my expectations and need to always be doing and achieving.

In the stillness of that summer, I discovered I loved lamp posts! I began a love affair with my once arch nemesis–tomatoes! I indulged in gelato every single day without an ounce of guilt. I discovered that I loved the smell of old churches, so I visited them as often as possible and I'm Jewish! I was finding *me*!

If you remember back when we started this trip together, I told you about the encounter I had with my very sassy seven-year-old self on top of that vortex in Sedona. I shared with you a little about our conversation and the way we left things. More importantly, I shared with you how I left her. Now that you and I are official road dawgs (pals), I want to share with you a bit more about the conversation I had with her.

As we sat together leaning up against those red rocks, I said to her, "I love you and I always will. I'm so sorry for what happened to you, but I can't keep protecting you and hiding you (behind all the weight) away trying to keep you safe. I can't keep worrying about you and not taking care of me." I then told her it was time for her to go off on her own and take care of herself and it was also time for me to do the same.

If you recall, I mentioned to you that when I left, I still felt like something was still missing. Something didn't feel quite right on that drive back to Los Angeles. While I sensed I felt a bit lighter, there was still something that felt off. But I did what I did best and tucked away that uncomfortable feeling hoping for it to just disappear.

And as you have probably witnessed in your own life, things don't just go away. If it's meant for you to heal, it will return again and again. Pushing your emotions and feelings down doesn't keep them hidden for long. The best thing you and I can do is choose to face them head on. The quicker we do that, the less crap we carry around.

On one of my last days in Italy before returning to the states, I was visiting my favorite church in Florence, San Miniato al Monte, in the very early morning. I loved to watch the morning sun peek through the beautiful stain glassed window in the back of that church. I loved the sound of the old floors creak as I walked upon them. When it's this early, nobody is there, so you can hear every sound the old building makes. At times, if I listened closely enough, I could hear the old church speaking to me. On this morning though, the church didn't speak to me.

God did.

There I was with my eyes closed, feeling the warmth from the sun through my favorite window, when I heard very clearly, "You weren't supposed to leave her, you were supposed to love her." My eyes popped open and I literally gasped. It was as if somebody had just socked me in the stomach with the truth. I knew exactly what was being told to me.

The message.

I hadn't even been thinking about Sedona—that moment—those years ago. I was simply taking in the last moments in my favorite church, wanting to hold on to all of what I had experienced these past few months and there it was—a truth bomb like I had never heard one before.

There was no doubt that *this* message, *this* church, *this* trip, *this* heartbreak, all had led me to *this* moment—*this truth*. There was no doubt that my seven-year-old self that I had separated from decades ago had shown back up in Sedona to reunite with me to make me whole again. *That* was what I had been feeling on the drive back home from Sedona. The reason I felt like something was missing was because there was something missing!

I left her sitting up there in her camp clothes on that mountaintop. I walked away from her when all she wanted from me was for me to love her again. She just wanted me to be there with her, to take care of her and not hide her or leave her. She just wanted me to truly open my arms to her.

You see, when that abuse happened to me, all I wanted was for someone (anyone) to say, "I'm sorry this happened to you. I'm sorry that someone wasn't there to protect you. I'm sorry that we messed up. That he messed up. It wasn't your fault. You didn't do anything wrong. I'm sorry that you had to go through this!" And then I wanted to be held and I wanted to cry my eyes out!

But I didn't get that. I didn't even know I needed that. The people in my life didn't know I needed that. But in that moment, on top of that crazy red rock, vortex healing thing, that is what she needed to hear from me and that is why she showed back up. Now in this church, I understood it all. *I wasn't supposed to leave her. I was supposed to love her.*

This is the message for *all* of us—for you. I know it's hard to sit with the wounds. It's hard to open yourself up and remain vulnerable. I know it's hard to put yourself out there and risk being hurt once again. But if you continue to remain separated from yourself, you will also continue to feel incomplete and lost. You will search the world over for something—someone—anything to fill that space within you that only *you* can.

Beautiful soul, you are always being called back to you. The wounded, scared, hurt part of yourself that you closed yourself off to long ago is always trying to get your attention. But are you listening or even ready? For me, I wasn't ready on that mountaintop in Sedona; but without a shadow of a doubt, that morning in that church, *I was ready.* (Truth be told, standing in a church 1000 years old while hearing the voice of God, one better make themselves ready!)

Every challenge you experience, every letdown and disappointment, every perceived failure and every roadblock–all of it is a blinking and blaring road sign that you are off course, off center and out of alignment. Yet we often curse it rather than receiving the true message lying within it.

What if we were all taught as kids that instead of trying to push through something, ignore it or be better than it, that we simply sit with it? What if we were taught to ask it questions?

"What have you come to show me?"
"What do you need me to see?"
"How can I grow?"

What if we were taught that unhappiness, anger, frustration, sadness, etc. aren't bad? What if we were taught that they are simply feelings that deserve acknowledgement, love and no judgement? We place so much emphasis on being happy and living a life of complete happiness that when we fail to do so, we beat ourselves up over it. We feel there is something wrong with us.

Now, I'm not saying that you and I shouldn't strive for a life that is more joyous and happier; but what I am saying is that we are human beings and the most beautiful thing about us is our ability to feel! It's our ability to experience and live a full-spectrum of emotions and a fabulous, technicolor-filled life that is comprised of *all* emotions.

What if *Loving Yourself Happy* is about loving yourself through *all* your emotions? Through the sadness, anger, self-doubt and fear. Maybe self-love and ultimately happiness is born through the kindness, gentleness and compassion you show yourself in the not-so-easy times. Maybe happiness is born through accepting *all* of you just as you are.

So, this is it? There's no magic pill to help me love myself happy?

I'm sorry—no. I simply don't have all the answers and anyone who tells you they do—run for the freaking hills! While I would really love to give you an exact formula to ever-lasting happiness, all I know and all I have learned is to simply show up for myself each day doing the best I can, loving the best I know how. On those days when I might fall short, love myself through those moments. Be kind and compassionate towards our imperfect selves and remember that we are all just trying to find our way.

Go easy on yourself.

This is your one life. Don't waste another minute of it thinking and wishing for something else. Your happy is right in front of you. It's in the dew on the flower, the squint in your eyes in the sunshine, the beating of your heart before a big presentation. It's in the butterflies in your stomach when you see the one you love and in the perfect peace you feel in the absolute stillness of moments. It's in the moments that don't always feel good but always, always have something to show you.

Love yourself patiently.
Love yourself more.
Love yourself full.
Love Yourself Happy.

This is the road trip, beautiful one. It's not about the destination on a map. It's about the detours and rest stops and refuels along the way. It's about the beautiful moments being appreciated and the challenging ones being appreciated even more. It's about moving through this life keeping your heart open and your soul untethered to any one outcome or expectation.

It's about learning to forgive yourself, laugh at yourself and take off on crazy adventures simply because your heart says *"GO!"*. It's about loving who you choose to travel through this life with, and finally, it's about returning to the one place that you stayed away from for so long—*you.*

WELCOME HOME, MY FRIEND.

Put the car in park.
Go inside.
Take your shoes off.
Stay awhile.

EPILOGUE

Oh, and in case you were wondering–I finally did have that reunion. I had that reunion back to me and to John, who is also now my fiancé. It's interesting the things that show up and come along when you feel whole again. I no longer needed him (or anyone or anything) to complete me. I had found my missing half and it was always staring back at me in the mirror.

So yeah, this crazy gal who loves her movie-themed life, found her very own happy ending. (Another spoiler: the journey and learning never really ends.)

While I have reunited back with my younger self, we spent so many years apart that it's still a 'getting to know you' time. Six years later and I'm still discovering my walls, my joys, my beliefs, expectations, opinions, etc. and guess what? I'm loving myself through them all with patience, compassion and understanding. And yes, I'm loving myself even through frustration and impatience.

You see, we don't just love ourselves happy. We love ourselves in and through it all. And in the doing so of that, happiness sits in your soul cradling you as you continue your journey through this life hand and hand with the one person that is and will always be your greatest love, *you.*

Before I go, one last thing…

I wish I could tell you that you will never have another difficulty again. I wish I could promise you only triumphs and joys and successes. But what I can promise you is that if you love yourself through it all, the good and the bad, then life will be that much sweeter and the journey that much easier.

So, don't forget to love the places within you that have been forgotten. Don't forget to awaken the spaces within you that you have allowed to fall asleep. Don't forget to greet the parts of you that you've turned away because it hurt too much to look at them.

And don't forget that all your cracks and crevices, wounds and holes deserve your love. Remember, you are whole and all of you needs to be loved.

You, beautiful soul, are worthy of your love. And you, beautiful soul, deserve a life that you love. Go forth dear one and love yourself blissfully, crazily and ridiculously happy. As a matter of fact, go ahead and love yourself through it all!

Okay, I lied—one more thing, Can I get one last PB&J for the road?

xo,
Shari

P.S. I can't wait to tell you about my 30-minute walk with love! Man, now *that* was a trip! Let me know when you're up for another one!

P.P.S. Psst—go easy on yourself.

ABOUT THE AUTHOR

Motivated by her own journey through childhood sexual abuse and other childhood traumas, Shari Alyse has spent her life learning how to love herself fully and completely. Shari helps women and men discover their joy by reconnecting them back to themselves through the practice of self-love. Shari is passionate about sharing her messages of self-love, self-acceptance, and joy as an Inspirational Speaker ("Joy Magnet"), Self-Love Coach, and Author.

Shari is also the Co-Founder of The Wellness Universe (www. TheWellnessUniverse.com), an online community and platform of holistic wellness practitioners and heart-based entrepreneurs whose mission it is to create a happy, healthy and whole world. She is the CIO (Chief Inspirational Officer) of Soul Ventures, Inc., a company focused on being a catalyst for positive change on the planet.

Shari's personal mission is to help you discover, embrace and love your YOU. She believes that your self-care ultimately is the world's care.

You can catch Shari's inspiration on her weekly podcast, The J-Spot, her daily videos on YouTube, Facebook and Instagram and meet her live at her workshops and retreats in Los Angeles and throughout the U.S.

"My idea of the perfect life is spent on planes, trains, and automobiles seeing the world. I dream of traveling the United States in an RV speaking to whomever will listen about self-love and self-hugs. In the meanwhile, if you're in the Los Angeles area, you can definitely find me on top of some mountain filming my motivational 'Hiking with Shari' series. My favorite part of the day is being greeted by the sun, the trees and God. I am grateful for the love that fills my heart and my passion for life that fills my soul. I want to squeeze out all the awesome that life has to offer!"

Shari lives in Los Angeles with her fiancé, John and their cats, Hershey and Piper.

Find out more about Shari and sign up for her JOY-letters here: www.ShariAlyse.com

APPRECIATION

First and foremost, thank you G.O.D. for loving me, guiding me and always being here for me. And also for being amused with all the different iterations of your name I've rapped to you each morning on our walks together. I hope you, the birds and bunnies have enjoyed it. I know I'm not always patient when it comes to my desires, but I do know that you've got me wrapped up tight like a Snuggie in your arms and you will deliver all that I need! I couldn't possibly be where I am right now without knowing how loved I am by you.

Mom and Dad: There isn't a day that goes by that I don't know how loved I am by you both. As I've become an adult, I know that being a parent is just another extension of yourself. You didn't get a handbook. You did your best and your best is more than enough because I am in love with who I am and that is only possible because of you both. THANK YOU. I love you more than I could ever express in words and you know I have a lot of those.

To my sister, Tami: Thank you for always being my biggest fan in anything that I do. Thank you for protecting me against my 6th grade boyfriend by giving him a black eye. It's important for you to know that I have NEVER blamed you for anything. You were my big sis and I only wanted to be around you. I love you and that has never wavered. Time to forgive yourself.

To my niece, Ariel: I can't wait to see how you will shift this world with your beautiful light! Please know the gift that you are. And to clear things up finally, I have moved aside to gift you with the throne.

To my family (both sides): I didn't always understand the importance of family, I just knew that you were there. And having someone 'there', is the most beautiful gift to give someone. Thank you for *always* being there and listening to me yap nonstop over the years. Thank you for helping to feed the entertainer in me by letting me perform for you over the years. You helped give me a confidence that I carry to the stages. I love you *all* with all of my heart.

Anna: My soul sister. My business partner. My best friend. You have been my biggest teacher. You have shown me parts of myself that I am so proud of and the other parts that I really needed to love and nurture more. I am honored to walk beside you in our 'little' venture to heal and change the world with The Wellness Universe. I'm inspired by your vision every day and I thank you for your confidence in me. I know you are so excited that this book is finally finished, but surprise!–there is already another one in the works! I love you. Thank you, Hugo!

WU Angels (Ashley, Jenny, Kim, Heather and L.E.): You are my heart. You are stronger and braver than anyone I know. Thank you for always cheering me on and keeping me uplifted each and everyday. There isn't anything I wouldn't do for you.

I feel so unbelievably grateful for the circle of friends around me that believe in me and support me. I can't believe how much I am loved. I don't know what I did to deserve this, but my heart is unbelievably filled. I wish I could list you all but if you're my friend, you know how much I love you. Plus, I have probably gushed over you so I'm speaking to YOU.

To all my restaurant friends I partied with in NYC & LA, those were some of the best times of my life! I couldn't possibly handle another all-nighter like that, but I certainly can sit back and smile remembering the conversations, laughs and occasional hook-ups.

Jasmin Terrany: My first 'real' therapist who taught me that I could love someone and still be angry at them. My emotions are valid. This permission to feel what I feel has changed my life.

Thank you to Neale Donald Walsch, Wayne Dyer, Abraham-Hicks, Iyanla Vanzant, Marianne Williamson, Dan Millman, and Elizabeth Gilbert for leading me through the darkness and out to the other side. Your words carried me and have inspired me to help light up the hearts of others. To every writer who has soothed my soul and aching heart, I thank you.

To Oprah: In 1981 when I was sexually abused, nobody was speaking about it. In 1986, you did. Thank you for making me feel less alone in the world. You made me want to be a talk show host to help change lives. Although you didn't choose me for your talk show host competition, I hold no grudges. *smile*

To the two angels disguised as secretaries or paralegals that played Barbies with me that day I testified against my abuser–immense gratitude for making that day feel as normal as humanly possible for me. For anyone who has ever thought that you have to cure a disease or end starvation to change the world, please know that showing up with a compassionate heart is enough to do that!

Thank you to all the angels and guides that have shown up in my life– those that I recognize and those that have yet to make your appearance. I have a mighty, mighty team and you all have a sh*tload of patience to keep showing up for me!

Thank you to my book coach, Lynda Goldman, who lovingly talked me out of the 'Gelato Chronicles' to share this book instead. I am grateful for your insight and guidance. And thank you to my editor, Elizabeth

Kipp, who reminded me that not everyone knows what's in my head so saying things like 'him' and 'it' might not always be clear. I'm forever grateful for our pact we made that day at Cafe Gratitude. We did it!

Thank you to anyone who has ever smiled at me, encouraged me, saw me, loved me and accepted me. You were a perfect example for me of how to treat myself.

To my John—I didn't know it was you the first time we met but what I did know was that I wanted to see you again. And after I saw you, after *every* time I saw you, I wanted to see you again. Then that one day in NYC on Columbus Avenue when you boldly grabbed my hand and I got a flash of us as an old couple, I knew then that I would no longer have to 'wish' to see you again, but that we would everyday for the rest of our lives. It wasn't an easy journey getting here, my love, and if I could go back in time, I would've kissed you that first day in my living room and not make you wait years for me to say 'I love you'. But hey, it makes for a great movie and you know I am all about my life being one great romance movie!

And finally, thank you to the beautiful and trusting seven-year-old who only wanted to be loved and hugged. Thank you for never giving up on and sticking by me even when I inadvertently pushed you aside. I love you with every part of me. I am proud of you and there isn't a day that goes by that I'm not grateful for you. We are stuck together forever. And guess what? Trusting people is still a beautiful thing! I vow to give you hugs forever.

PLEASE LEAVE
A REVIEW

Thank you so much for taking the time to read *Love Yourself Happy!* I certainly hope it lit your soul up! If it did, I would be so honored and appreciative if you would hop on over to Amazon and leave me a review. Thank you in advance for lighting *me* up!

Smiles,
Shari

WORK WITH SHARI

To book Shari for interviews or to speak at your event, please email:
Shari@ShariAlyse.com

"Shari's energy and commitment to her audience is unparalleled. If you're looking to learn, grow, and laugh, Shari is the perfect keynote for you."

— Bert Oliva, Leadership Expert &
International Orator

"Having seen Shari Alyse speak in person on several occasions on different topics, I can say I am always moved by the experience. Shari pulls us into her life and story with her unapologetically real, raw and moving stories meant to help the audience transition to a higher sense of self and empowerment. Shari makes you feel like you are not alone in your plight, whatever it may be. Highly relatable and leaving a lasting impression. Shari truly motivates with her heartfelt talks. Be ready to be a bit uncomfortable, be ready to laugh and be ready to shed a tear when you attend a talk that Shari puts all of her heart and soul into."

— Anna Pereira, Founder of The Wellness Universe

"What you shared last night with that room of women was life changing. Not only do you "hear" them, you "see" them. Giving women your wisdom uplifted the women in that room and gave them a structure to pull them selves up and it gave them hope."

— Cheryl Meyer, Award-winning
Author & Health Coach

"Shari is an amazing, entertaining, educational, and engaging presenter!"

— L.E. Saba, Registered Holistic Nutritionist,
Environmental Health Specialist

Shari has created a 12 week one-on-one Self-Love coaching program, 'Love Yourself Happy', based on the concepts from this book. If you're interested in working with Shari as your Self-Love coach & guide, you can connect with her at www.ShariAlyse.com

"Shari brings out the best of people. Working with Shari was the best decision ever. It opened the doors for me to show up as my authentic self more than ever and helped me grow as human being till this day. Thank you, Shari, for sharing your wisdom and keeping my body, mind and soul in balance! She has motivated me to spread my love wings and to share the best version of myself."

— Jessica Klosa

"I was diagnosed with a rare condition that restricts me from leaving my home and I had never felt so lost and unsure of myself and my future. I thought I had reached my fullest potential so to speak, but thanks to Shari and the techniques she has taught me, I feel empowered with a renewed sense of purpose. Shari helped rekindle my gratitude for life, reignited my passion for writing, and really deepened the love and acceptance of myself.

– Jenny Tasker

"Shari gave me the tools I needed when I was down to rebuild my self- confidence, self- respect, courage and overall greatness to conquer my fears and obstacles. This doesn't happen overnight and it doesn't happen unless you put the work in. That's what Shari is there for. Shari will change your life and you will start to live the life you dream of."

– Tarriss Saurer

Made in the USA
Las Vegas, NV
15 September 2022

55351186R00125